Max Stone

The Book of Metatron
The Angel of the Presence

Copyright
Original Title: O Livro de Metatron: O Anjo da Presença
Copyright © 2024, published by Luiz Antonio dos Santos ME.

This book explores the transcendent presence and unique role of Metatron, the archangel who serves as a bridge between the Creator and creation. Examining Enoch's transformation into Metatron and his role as a celestial scribe, spiritual guide and guardian of knowledge, the book reveals the divine secrets and impact of this archangel on the lives of the faithful.

2nd edition
Production Team
Author: Max Stone
Proofreader: Virginia Moreira dos Santos
Graphic design and layout: Arthur Mendes da Costa
Cover: Anderson Casagrande Neto
Translator: Gabriel Massada

Publication and identification
Metatron / by Max Stone

Booklas Publishing, 2024
Categories: Religion / Philosophy / Body, Mind and Spirit
DDC: 231 - CDU: 24-52
All rights reserved:
Booklas Publishing / Luiz Antonio dos Santos ME
No part of this book may be reproduced, stored in a retrieval system, or transmitted in any form or by any means, electronic, mechanical, photocopying, recording, or otherwise, without the prior permission of the copyright holder.

Summary

Preface 4
Chapter One Divine Origin 6
Chapter Two The Voice of God 17
Chapter Three Guardian of Knowledge 27
Chapter Four The Midwayer 38
Chapter Five Attributed Miracles 48
Chapter Six The Cult of Metatron 58
Chapter Seven Spiritual Practices 69
Chapter Eight Metatron's Protection 79
Chapter Nine Metatron and Healing 87
Chapter Ten Spiritual Enlightenment 94
Chapter Eleven Spiritual Teachings 102
Chapter Twelve Dimensions 109
Chapter Thirteen The Archangel and Humanity 116
Chapter Fourteen Metatron's Teachings 124
Chapter Fifteen Esoteric Sciences 132
Chapter Sixteen Contemporary Challenges 140
Chapter Seventeen Metatron's Eternal Legacy 148
Chapter Eighteen Techniques of Communication 155
Chapter Nineteen Prayers and Rituals 168
Epilogue 180

Preface

Metatron, the archangel at the heart of the divine, radiates wisdom and power. His light illuminates the celestial spheres and serves as a mediator between the Creator and creation. Metatron's presence is a testament to the closeness between the human and the divine, a beacon of hope and light for all who seek to elevate their souls.

This book, The Book of Metatron, is not just a literary work, but a journey of transformation where history and spirituality unite to reveal the ultimate purpose of this extraordinary archangel.Each chapter unveils layers of occult knowledge, exploring the origins of the prophet Enoch, his ascension to heavenly status and his metamorphosis into the archangel Metatron. Metatron is the keeper of divine secrets, the voice of God and the guide of souls. He offers healing, protection and wisdom to those who seek to understand the greater purpose of their lives. Be inspired by Metatron's presence. His stories and transcendental teachings will illuminate your spiritual journey, guide you through life's challenges and reveal the transformative power of faith.Metatron spreads his wings over you, offering protection, healing and a clear vision of the path to enlightenment.Open your mind, open your heart and allow Metatron to reveal to you the mysteries of the universe. This is more than a book - it's a call to transcendence.Welcome to the kingdom of Metatron.

Chapter One
Divine Origin

In a realm beyond the reach of the stars and older than time itself, there exists a being whose existence is both a mystery and a wonder. Known as Metatron, this archangel occupies a unique position in the heavenly choir, serving as a bridge between the Creator and creation. His story is rich, woven with threads of faith, power and eternal wisdom. His origins, though shrouded in mystery, are often discussed in sacred scriptures and esoteric texts, offering glimpses of his rise to celestial status.

Metatron is often identified as the most powerful of the archangels, a being whose name means "he who sits beside the divine throne". His presence is synonymous with power and divine nearness, qualities that make him a figure of immense respect and reverence in the Judeo-Christian tradition. He is said to have been resurrected from his mortal form - some say he was the prophet Enoch, transformed and taken to heaven to serve God after a life of faithfulness and virtue.

Enoch's transformation into Metatron is a story of transcendence and divine reward. According to apocryphal texts such as the Book of Enoch, God was so impressed by his integrity and piety that he decided to take him to heaven. There he was transformed into an angelic being, endowed with wisdom and powers beyond human comprehension. This transformation is not only a testament to God's love and mercy, but also an eternal sign of what is possible for the truly faithful.

As an archangel, Metatron has many responsibilities. One of his most important functions is that of a celestial scribe, recording all the actions and events of the universe. He is said to have a profound knowledge of divine laws and the inner workings of creation, knowledge that is recorded in the 'Book of Life', a celestial compilation of all souls and their deeds.

In addition to his role as scribe, he acts as an advisor to other celestial beings and as an intercessor for human prayer. His ability to mediate between heaven and earth is one of the reasons why he is so revered. He is seen as a spiritual guide, someone who can offer wisdom and guidance both in times of need and in matters of spiritual development.

Stories about this archangel also emphasise his proximity to the divine throne. He is often described as being at the right hand of God, a position that symbolises his importance and proximity to the supreme power. This privileged position makes Metatron one of the few beings who can endure the immediate presence of God without being consumed; he is a direct witness to divine omnipotence.

Metatron's origin and his role in the cosmos are subjects of great fascination and deep respect. His story is a reminder of divine love and the reward that awaits those who are faithful. As an archangel who serves as a bridge between God and man, he remains a powerful symbol of intercession and heavenly authority, a beacon of hope and protection for all who seek the divine light.

In spiritual belief, few figures are as shrouded in mystery and majesty as Metatron. This archangel serves not only as God's scribe, but also as an inexhaustible source of celestial wisdom. The depth of his knowledge is so vast that even other celestial beings often seek his advice on matters of great importance. It is through these interactions that Metatron exemplifies his nature as a mediator, not only between God and man, but also between the various orders of angels.

One of the most intriguing aspects is his association with mysticism. In particular, the Kabbalistic tradition portrays him as the angel who guides mortals through the celestial spheres, offering enlightenment and spiritual understanding. The Kabbalah, an esoteric school of Jewish thought, describes Metatron as the one who sits at the top of the Tree of Life, a symbol representing all aspects of existence. His position in this spiritual hierarchy testifies to his role as a facilitator of divine understanding and as a bridge to a deeper understanding of creation and human purpose.

Metatron is also described as the guardian of cosmic equilibrium. He is often associated with the balance between mercy and judgement, a recurring theme in theologies that seek to explain the dualistic nature of God. In this role, he not only transmits the divine will, but also ensures that all actions and events in the universe are recorded and judged according to the eternal laws established by the Creator.

In addition to his spiritual and administrative functions, the Archangel is revered for his accessibility to the faithful. Unlike other archangels, whose presence may be more distant or shrouded in celestial formality, he is seen as an accessible mentor, a guide who understands human tribulations and offers advice and comfort. This characteristic makes him a central figure in many devotional practices, in which the faithful seek his intercession for personal and spiritual matters.

The cult of Metatron, although not as widespread as that of other archangels such as Michael or Gabriel, has its own richness, especially among those who engage in mystical studies. He is often invoked in rituals that seek spiritual purification or protection from evil forces. These practices usually involve elaborate invocations, using sigils and holy names to attract the archangel's attention and gain his favour.

For those who study the sacred texts, his figure offers a direct link to the divine. He is the herald who announces hidden truths, revealing them to those who deserve them and concealing them from those who are not yet ready to receive such revelations. His role as guardian of sacred knowledge is perhaps one of his most important aspects, for it is through him that knowledge of divine laws and the universe is kept alive and passed down from generation to generation.

This reverence for Metatron is widely reflected in spiritual literature, where he is often cited as an example of celestial virtue and divine commitment. His legacy is a testament to the power of faith and the eternal human desire to connect with the sacred. In him, the faithful find not only a guide, but a guardian of spiritual truth whose influence transcends the barriers between heaven and earth.

As we explore Metatron's vast role in the cosmos, we discover his intrinsic connection to critical moments in human history. Known as the 'Eye of God', he is often portrayed as a witness to human actions, from the simplest acts of kindness to the most tumultuous episodes of transgression. His role as a heavenly witness and recorder implies an almost unimaginable omnipresence, present in all the places and moments in which the divine chooses to intervene or observe.

One of the most fascinating stories about Metatron is his participation in the giving of the Ten

Commandments to Moses on Mount Sinai. It is said that Metatron acted as a mediator, helping to facilitate communication between God and Moses. This story vividly illustrates his role as a divine messenger, a bridge between the heavenly and the earthly, able to bring God's word to humanity in a way that could be understood and followed.

Metatron is also associated with the Tree of Life, a Kabbalistic symbol representing the ten spheres (sefirot) of knowledge and existence. He is often seen as the guardian of this sacred knowledge, guiding scholars and mystics on their spiritual journeys through the intricacies of the Kabbalah. Through his guidance, those seeking spiritual truth can navigate the many layers of understanding and enlightenment.

In addition to his position as an entity of wisdom and knowledge, he is revered for his ability to understand and mediate human emotions. He is seen as a comforter of the afflicted, offering hope and guidance to those facing spiritual or earthly challenges. His interventions are described as moments of profound transformation in which believers feel a renewal of faith and a strengthening of their connection with the divine.

His influence is also found in different cultures and faiths, adapting to the spiritual needs of different times and peoples. In some traditions he is regarded as the angel of death, guiding the souls of the deceased to the afterlife. In other traditions, he is a celestial warrior who fights the forces of evil to maintain order and peace in the universe. This versatility of his functions highlights his importance as a central figure in angelic theology and his ability to serve God in a variety of roles.

His relationship with other angels is also of great interest. He is often seen working with and leading legions of angels in various celestial tasks and missions. Through his interactions with other celestial beings, he not only carries out God's plans, but also helps to maintain harmony and order among the angelic hosts.

Metatron's presence in the lives of the faithful is a constant reminder of God's love and care. His appearances and interventions are seen as divine signs, moments when heaven touches earth. For those who dedicate their lives to the study and veneration of this powerful archangel, he is a mentor, a protector and, above all, a constant link with the divine.

As we delve deeper into the mystical aspects of Metatron's existence, we find his significant role in the sacred scriptures. One of the most profound texts associated with Metatron is the "Sefer Ha-Razim", or Book of Mysteries, which supposedly contains the secrets of the universe revealed to him directly by God. This book serves as a guide for those seeking to understand the deeper, esoteric meanings of existence and provides a framework for mystical practices and spiritual exploration.

Metatron's association with the Book of Mysteries highlights his role as a teacher of divine wisdom. It is believed that through this text he teaches deserving souls about the structure of the cosmos, the dynamics of creation and the paths to spiritual enlightenment. His teachings are not for the casual seeker, but are reserved for those who have proven their devotion and are ready to ascend to higher levels of spiritual understanding.

Mystical traditions also emphasise his role in the process of divine creation itself. According to these teachings, Metatron was involved in the formation of the universe, acting under God's direction. He is sometimes referred to as the "Lesser YHVH", a title that denotes a reflection of God's own essence, imbued with the power to participate in the act of creation. This aspect of his identity adds a layer of complexity to his character, portraying him not only as a messenger or intercessor, but also as a co-creator, shaping the very fabric of reality alongside the Almighty.

In spiritual circles, Metatron is often invoked during meditative and ritualistic practices aimed at personal transformation and the attainment of a higher consciousness. Practitioners believe that by connecting with the archangel they can access the divine energies necessary for personal growth and enlightenment. Their guidance is sought by making protective amulets, performing cleansing rituals and seeking prophetic visions. The associated rituals usually involve specific prayers, chants and the use of sacred geometry, which are believed to resonate with his essence and facilitate a deeper connection with the divine.

Metatron's influence extends beyond the spiritual realm; his presence is also felt in the more practical aspects of existence. He is considered the patron of life's various transitions, overseeing moments of significant change such as birth, marriage and even death. At each of these stages he offers his guidance and protection, ensuring that those under his care are protected from spiritual harm and aligned with their greater purpose.

In addition, his reach is said to include the oversight of other celestial beings. Legends speak of his role in educating young angels and imparting wisdom to the celestial hosts. This educational aspect of his mission is vital, as it ensures that divine knowledge and commands are accurately transmitted throughout the celestial hierarchy, thus maintaining order and harmony in the heavens.

From his mystical teachings to his involvement in divine creation, from his guidance in human affairs to his oversight of the celestial beings, Metatron embodies the many ways in which the divine interacts with the cosmos. His story is one not only of power and proximity to the divine, but also of responsibility and service, making him a truly exceptional figure in the pantheon of celestial beings.

He is not only an archangel who intercedes with God on behalf of humanity, but also a symbol of hope and spiritual connection. Those who worship him firmly believe that Metatron has the ability to open paths to a deeper understanding of the universe and to facilitate clearer communication with the divine.

Metatron is often seen as a portal to the divine, a window through which the finite can glimpse the infinite. His unique position as one of the beings closest to God gives him extraordinary authority and power, and it is this closeness that makes him such a powerful intercessor. According to many accounts, he is the most accessible of the archangels to those seeking divine wisdom, acting as a mentor and guide to those who wish to deepen their knowledge and spirituality.

His relationship with humans is also characterised by his ability to understand the complexities of earthly life. He is not a distant observer; on the contrary, he becomes involved in human affairs, offering his guidance and protection. In many esoteric traditions he is invoked in times of great uncertainty or difficulty, when his wisdom and power are sought to overcome adversity and find solutions.

Metatron is also known for his ability to purify and energise places and people. His presence is considered purifying, able to cleanse negativity and strengthen spiritual bonds. Cleansing and blessing rituals usually invoke his name, asking him to bring his purifying light into rooms and hearts.

The worship of Metatron crosses boundaries and finds a place in various religious and spiritual traditions. His figure is a bridge between ancient knowledge and modern practice, between the great celestial truths and the personal quest for growth and understanding. For many, Metatron is not just an archangel; he is a symbol of the human potential to transcend the visible and touch the eternal.

Each aspect of his existence reveals more about the structure of spirituality and how celestial beings can influence and enrich our lives.

With this understanding of Metatron, we are ready to embark on the next phases of our journey, exploring his interactions, teachings and specific impact on history and the spiritual lives of individuals around the world.

Chapter Two
The Voice of God

At the centre of scripture and mystical traditions, Metatron is revered not only as a divine messenger, but as the very voice of God. His function as the bearer of divine words places him in a unique position, acting as the channel through which the Creator's decrees are communicated to the world.

Since ancient times, the figure of the celestial messenger has played a central role in the world's religions. However, Metatron's unparalleled closeness to the Divine makes him unique among these beings. It is said that his voice carries the weight and authority of God, making his words not just messages but manifestations of divine thought. Those who recognise and respond to him are usually those who reach great depths of spiritual understanding and realisation.

One of the most significant episodes illustrating his ability to convey the divine will is his interaction with the prophet Moses mentioned earlier. In addition to his role on Mount Sinai, he also guided Moses on his journey to lead the Israelites out of Egypt. The

Scriptures report that he not only guided Moses, but also provided him with advice and knowledge that was fundamental to his mission.

His ability to act as counsellor and guide reflects his multifaceted nature. He is not simply a transmitter of commandments; he becomes deeply involved with those he serves, ensuring that divine messages are understood and properly implemented. This aspect of his service is crucial, as it ensures that God's will is not only heard, but actually carried out on Earth.

Metatron's voice is fundamental to the celebrations and rituals that honour his connection with the Divine. In many esoteric traditions it is a common practice to recite the words he is said to have spoken or transmitted in order to invoke his presence and blessing. These practices show that his voice is more than symbolic; it is an active force in spiritual practice, a source of power and protection. He is also often associated with the revelation of divine secrets. He is seen as a master who unlocks the secrets of the universe for those who are ready to receive them. This facet of his personality is particularly valued by mystics and spiritual scholars, who look to his revelations for a deeper understanding of spiritual and material reality.

The Archangel is therefore not only the voice of God, but an active participant in the spiritual dynamics of the world. He shapes, guides and influences the paths of humanity through his unique ability to directly communicate the essence of the Divine. His role as the voice of God is therefore fundamental not only to biblical events, but to the continuity of the spiritual tradition through the ages.

As we explore his role as the voice of God, we find his influence in the scriptures of various traditions. He not only transmits God's words, but also ensures that they are properly received and understood by the recipients, be they prophets, saints or simple believers. His ability to adapt the divine message to the needs and understandings of each age is evidence of his deep connection to the Creator and to creation.

In the context of the Kabbalistic tradition, he is often associated with the concept of "Logos" or the Word of God, a principle at the centre of creation and the maintenance of the universe. This concept emphasises the idea that words have power, and no one understands or manipulates this power better than Metatron. It is through his voice that orders are established, laws are formulated and harmony is maintained both in the heavens and on earth.

One of his most fascinating facets is his involvement in the training and guidance of the other angels. Considered one of the most enlightened angels, he often takes on the role of instructor to the celestial hosts, teaching them the intricacies of divine laws and how best to serve humanity. This educational function also extends to human beings, especially those who seek a deeper understanding of spiritual mysteries.

Mystical texts describe him as holding the keys to the heavenly portals, controlling access to realms of knowledge and experience beyond human comprehension. He acts not only as a messenger, but also as a guardian of divine secrets, carefully selecting who should receive which secrets based on their purity and purpose of heart. This selectivity ensures that the power of the divine words is not misused or misinterpreted.

Metatron is also known for appearing during critical events in human history, occasions when his words have served as guides or warnings. In several apocryphal tales he appears at moments of great crisis or decision, offering his wisdom and guidance. These encounters underline his importance as a mediator between God and man, emphasising his vital role in guiding the course of human history according to divine plans.

His voice is therefore one of authority, wisdom and compassion. He speaks not only to command or instruct, but also to comfort and console. For believers, he is a constant reminder of God's care and attention to his creations. His presence and words are a beacon of hope and guidance, lighting the way for those who seek to draw closer to the Divine. As we continue to explore his multifaceted existence, we see that his voice is a bridge between the eternal and the ephemeral, between the divine and the human, carrying truths that have the power to transform souls and shape destinies.

Though imbued with celestial authority, Metatron's voice is also known for its ability to inspire and renew faith in the hearts of the faithful. His ability to touch souls is not simply a matter of conveying messages; it is an art of combining the divine with the mundane, the eternal with the immediate.

He is often described in spiritual narratives as a comforter of the afflicted. His encounters with people usually occur in times of great need or despair. In these moments, his voice not only conveys messages from God, but also offers a presence that is reassuring and invigorating. He offers a kind of spiritual balm, a salve for souls wounded by the wear and tear of the material world.

As well as being a comforter, he is also a guide for the lost. There are countless accounts of people who, in moments of uncertainty or spiritual searching, have found direction and purpose through an encounter, whether in vision or meditation, with this powerful archangel. His voice in these encounters serves as a beacon, guiding seekers through the mists of doubt and fear to a deeper understanding of their own place in the divine plan.

One remarkable aspect is his ability to speak in terms that are both universal and intimate. He doesn't just speak to crowds; he speaks to individuals, addressing their specific needs and unique circumstances. This ability to personalise the message makes him an extremely effective intermediary between God and man, ensuring that divine messages are not only heard, but truly understood and internalised.

Metatron also plays a crucial role at times of great spiritual transition or revelation. In various traditions, he is the archangel who announces significant changes or imminent events that will have a profound effect on the world order or the spiritual progress of humanity. His words on these occasions are both warnings and announcements, designed to prepare his listeners for what is to come and to encourage them to remain steadfast in their faith.

In addition to his role as messenger and guide, his voice is also a source of teaching and wisdom. He is known for his profound teachings on the nature of the universe, the laws of creation and the paths to spiritual enlightenment. For mystics and scriptural scholars, his words are an invaluable resource, full of insights that can be studied and contemplated for a lifetime.

Through all these roles as comforter, guide, herald and teacher, Metatron shapes the spiritual experience of countless believers. His voice is more than mere communication; it is a manifestation of divine grace, touching those who hear it with a power that can alter the course of life and awaken souls to the higher reality of divine love and purpose.

The depth and breadth with which he fulfils his role as the Voice of God is visible not only in the great spiritual narratives, but also in the daily lives of the people who seek his intercession. He is not a remote figure, but a constant presence, readily accessible to those who call upon him with sincerity and purity of heart.

In many spiritual communities it is common to find individuals and groups who devote significant parts of their prayer and meditation practices to Metatron. They believe that through these practices they can establish a more direct connection with the Archangel, facilitating a dialogue that strengthens their faith and clarifies their spiritual journeys. Invocations in this context usually include requests for clarity, protection and wisdom.

Prayers to Metatron are particularly powerful, as he has the ability to present the believer's petitions directly to God. These prayers usually follow specific formulas that resonate with his energy, using words and phrases that are believed to evoke his presence. The result is a prayer practice that not only seeks intercession, but also a deeper communion with the divine through his figure.

In addition to prayer practices, Metatron is also a central figure in many forms of spiritual meditation. Guided meditations involving him are designed to help practitioners access higher levels of consciousness. During these sessions, meditators often report experiences of profound spiritual insight and visionary encounters with him, which help them to better understand their lives and the spiritual challenges they face.

The Archangel is also seen as a spiritual protector, defending those who invoke him against negative influences and spiritual dangers. Many devotees wear amulets or insignia representing him, believing that these objects are blessed with his protection. These amulets are particularly popular with those facing major life decisions or changes, as they believe he can offer not only protection but also divine guidance.

Metatron's influence on the daily activities of his followers is a testament to his accessibility and ongoing commitment to guiding humanity. He is not just a figure to be invoked in moments of crisis or during formal rituals; he is a constant guide, a mentor for all hours. For many, his presence in their lives is a source of comfort and strength, a constant reminder that the Divine is always within reach and attentive to their needs.

As his voice echoes throughout the cosmos, his influence extends far beyond spoken or transmitted words; it permeates the hearts and souls of those who seek a true connection with the Divine.

Metatron is celebrated not only as a messenger or intercessor, but as a symbol of God's ongoing presence in the world. His messages and interventions are seen as direct acts of divine guidance, offered not only in times of need, but as an ongoing part of the dialogue between heaven and earth. This perspective makes him a central figure in the daily spiritual practices of many devotees, integrating him deeply into their lives as a constant guide and protector.

His influence is also crucial to theological development within different traditions. Theologians and scriptural scholars often turn to the stories and teachings associated with Metatron to better understand the mysterious aspects of the faith. His actions and words are the subject of intense study and reflection, as they offer valuable insights into the ways in which the divine interacts with the material world.

The figure of Metatron also serves as a bridge to ecumenism within spiritual communities. Appearing in different religious traditions, he acts as a point of connection between different faiths, promoting a wider understanding and appreciation of the different ways in which people experience the sacred. This ability to unite different traditions around a common figure is one of the reasons why he remains such a powerful and respected presence in the spiritual world.

The celebrations and festivals dedicated to him in different cultures highlight his role as a source of inspiration and spiritual renewal. During these events, stories of his interventions are shared, teachings are discussed and prayers are offered, all in honour of the archangel who serves as the closest link between humanity and the divine. These celebrations not only strengthen individual beliefs, but also the community through the sharing of spiritual beliefs and experiences.

Ultimately, as the voice of God, Metatron is a beacon of hope and a symbol of the divine promise of closeness and care. For those who worship him, he is not just an archangel; he is a vital aspect of God's presence on earth, a constant reminder that the voice of the Divine is never far away and that heavenly guidance is always within reach for those who seek it with sincere hearts and open minds.

Chapter Three
Guardian of Knowledge

Archangel Metatron has many facets, and one of the most revered is his role as Guardian of Knowledge. This role not only reinforces his connection to the Divine, but also highlights his importance as one of the main Archangels responsible for the preservation and transmission of sacred knowledge throughout the ages.

From the beginning he has been associated with the concept of Eternal Knowledge. In esoteric traditions it is common to find references to this angel presiding over all the celestial archives where all the events of the universe are recorded. This celestial library is not merely a repository of facts, but a living collection of universal truths, divine laws and moral precepts. With its unparalleled access to these records, it is believed to play a crucial role in maintaining order and justice throughout the cosmos.

Her role as guardian of knowledge is multifaceted. She not only protects this sacred information, but also ensures that it is accessible to those who are worthy of it. This access is not granted lightly; it requires a sincere search and a willingness to live by divine principles. Therefore, she also acts as a judge of character, discerning which souls are ready to receive secrets that have been kept for millennia.

One of the most fascinating aspects of Metatron's role in the realm of knowledge is his interaction with mystics and sages throughout history. He is said to have appeared in dreams and visions to those deeply seeking spiritual understanding, offering guidance and insights that are sometimes coded and symbolic. These revelations usually require careful interpretation, but always serve to lead the recipient to greater spiritual growth and understanding.

In addition to his presence in the heavenly realms, he is known to influence intellectual and spiritual development on earth. He is seen as the patron of scholars and educators, inspiring those who dedicate their lives to spreading knowledge and truth. It is believed that his influence can be felt in libraries, classrooms and places of meditation where knowledge is highly valued and sought after.

Metatron is also credited with the authorship of sacred and esoteric texts, some of which describe the deepest structures of the universe and the spiritual forces that shape reality. These texts, although shrouded in mystery, are considered vital tools for those dedicated to spiritual study. They provide a map for navigating the complexities of the cosmos and for better understanding the connection between the spiritual and the material.

As the Guardian of Knowledge, he cements his position as one of the most powerful and respected figures in the celestial pantheon. His responsibility to maintain the integrity of divine knowledge is not merely a duty, but an expression of his fundamental nature. He is essentially the link between eternal knowledge and those who seek to transcend worldly understanding, guiding them towards the light of universal truth.

Metatron's ability to preserve and disseminate sacred knowledge is complemented by his unique ability to mediate between the divine and the earthly, making him a vital link in the chain of spiritual transmission. He not only preserves knowledge, but also facilitates its understanding and practical application, helping humanity to achieve greater harmony with universal laws.

He is often seen as the archangel of life and writing, the patron of scribes and scholars who dedicate their lives to the study of the sacred scriptures. This association highlights his central role in promoting spiritual study and understanding. For those who study the sacred texts, his influence is a constant source of inspiration and revelation.

One of the most intriguing elements of his role as guardian of knowledge is his association with the 'Shiur

Qomah', a mystical text detailing the dimensions of the divine body. This text is an example of the depth of esoteric knowledge he can reveal to the initiated. It describes the complexities of the cosmos in a poetic and deeply symbolic way, offering scholars a unique insight into the structure of the universe.

In addition to texts and scriptures, he also plays a crucial role in overseeing spiritual learning through dreams and visions. He is able to use these altered states of consciousness as vehicles to convey important messages and lessons, usually in the form of parables or allegories. These communications are particularly valued for their ability to inspire deep insight and personal transformation.

Metatron is also recognised for his ability to unravel mysteries beyond the reach of ordinary human understanding. In various traditions he is regarded as the master of celestial secrets, possessing knowledge not only of the workings of the divine, but also of the interactions between cosmic and earthly forces. This knowledge enables him to help those who seek not only spiritual enlightenment, but also a deeper understanding of the laws of nature and their relationship to the divine.

His role as an educator and spiritual guide is a testament to his dedication not only to preserving knowledge, but also to developing wisdom in others. He doesn't keep the keys to knowledge to himself; he offers them to those who show a genuine desire to learn and grow. This openness transforms knowledge into a living tool, a resource that enriches and uplifts those touched by its wisdom.

As the guardian of knowledge, Metatron plays a vital role not only in the heavens but also on earth, influencing the intellectual and spiritual development of humanity. He is a powerful symbol of the intersection of the divine and the earthly, a bridge between the ethereal and the material, guiding seekers on their path to true enlightenment.

His profound understanding of divine and cosmic laws makes him an essential figure not only in the celestial hierarchies, but also in the earthly quest for spiritual wisdom. His guardianship of sacred knowledge includes not only the preservation but also the active dissemination of this wisdom, ensuring that it reaches those who are ready to receive and understand its depth.

In many spiritual narratives he is depicted as orchestrating the flow of knowledge from the divine realm to the human world through a series of complex and interconnected channels. He directs these flows with an expert hand, ensuring that the knowledge distributed is appropriate to the level of spiritual maturity of the recipients. This careful management prevents the misuse of sacred knowledge and maintains the balance between revelation and mystery.

One of his most notable functions is his involvement in the initiation and training of other celestial beings. As a teacher and mentor to younger or less experienced angels, he imparts the wisdom they need to fulfil their duties effectively. This educational role is crucial to maintaining the order and functionality of the celestial realms, ensuring that all beings within them understand their roles and the divine laws they must uphold.

On Earth, his influence is often felt in places dedicated to learning and spiritual exploration, such as temples, monasteries and spiritual retreat centres. He is regarded as the patron of these places, giving them an atmosphere conducive to deep contemplation and the search for wisdom. Devotees and seekers who visit these places often report feelings of deep peace and clarity, attributes that facilitate their spiritual journeys.

He is also associated with the protection of ancient texts and artefacts containing esoteric knowledge. It is believed that he watches over these items, ensuring that they are properly preserved and passed on from generation to generation. This role is linked to his wider function as guardian of the continuum of spiritual knowledge, linking past, present and future in an eternal chain of enlightenment.

He also plays a significant role at times of intellectual or spiritual breakthrough. Historically, when significant advances in understanding or crucial revelations have occurred, many have attributed these moments to his guidance or intervention. His ability to inspire and catalyse change testifies to his deep involvement not only with the celestial but also with the human quest for knowledge.

Beyond the boundaries of traditional learning, his guidance extends into the realm of innovation and creative thinking. He is seen as a kind of muse, inspiring artists, writers and thinkers to push the boundaries of conventional understanding and explore new ideas that resonate with the sacred truths he holds. This aspect shows that sacred knowledge is not static, but constantly evolving and expanding through human experience and perception.

As the guardian of knowledge, Metatron embodies the dynamic interaction between the eternal and the temporal, the divine and the mundane. His role ensures that sacred wisdom is not a relic of the past, but a living, breathing element of present and future human experience. Through him, the path to enlightenment is kept alive, inviting all who are willing to embark on a journey of profound transformation and discovery.

Metatron's role as Guardian of Knowledge encompasses not only the protection and transmission of esoteric wisdom, but also the facilitation of spiritual connections between different realms. His unique position allows him to act as a bridge between the divine and the mundane, offering guidance and enlightenment to those seeking deeper understanding and spiritual growth.

One of the most mystical aspects of his guidance is his connection to the Akashic Records, which are believed to contain all universal events, thoughts, words, emotions and intentions that have occurred in the past, present or will occur in the future. These records are a cosmic book of each soul's journey through time, and he is often described as the guardian of this repository. By providing access to these records, he helps people understand their personal history and the karmic patterns that shape their lives.

In addition to his custodial functions, he is also seen as a spiritual catalyst, capable of activating or heightening an individual's spiritual awareness. This is particularly important for those on the path of Ascension or seeking to raise their consciousness to higher levels of understanding. Her energy is said to help clear psychic and spiritual blockages, allowing a clearer channel for the flow of divine energy.

His presence is often invoked during meditative practices designed to expand spiritual perception and access higher dimensions of consciousness. Practitioners of various mystical traditions may use specific invocations or mantras to seek his assistance in their spiritual practices. It is believed that these invocations help to align the seeker's vibrational frequency with his, making it easier to receive his guidance and wisdom.

Metatron's guidance is also crucial for those involved in inter-dimensional travel or exploring the astral plane. His knowledge of cosmic pathways and dimensions allows him to guide souls through these often confusing and labyrinthine terrains, ensuring that their spiritual journeys are safe and enlightening.

He is also a figure of immense compassion and empathy, essential qualities in his role as educator and guide. He understands the challenges faced by those seeking enlightenment and offers support that is both empowering and stimulating. This compassionate guidance makes him not only a teacher, but also a spiritual guide and protector.

Metatron's teachings, usually communicated through symbols and energetic transmissions, are not limited to language or conventional forms. They can manifest as sudden insights, dreams or even synchronistic events that deliver messages and lessons in the most unexpected ways. These teachings are tailored to the spiritual needs of the individual, ensuring that they are relevant and transformative.

In essence, his guardianship of spiritual knowledge and wisdom is a multidimensional endeavour that spans time, space and consciousness. His role as educator, protector and guide contributes significantly to the spiritual evolution of the individual and humanity as a whole. Through his efforts, the sacred wisdom of all times is not only preserved, but made accessible to those who seek to explore the depths of their own souls and the mysteries of the universe.

Metatron actively engages with those on a spiritual journey, offering not only knowledge, but profound insight and support for personal and collective growth. He challenges, provokes and encourages spiritual seekers to question and expand their understanding. His interventions aim to catalyse growth and inspire transformation, making him a dynamic force in the spiritual evolution of individuals and groups. Through dreams, visions and meditative experiences, he communicates in a deeply personal and transformative way, ensuring that the lessons he imparts are not only understood, but integrated into a person's spiritual practice.

Metatron's guardianship also involves the delicate task of balancing revealed knowledge with the mysteries that must remain hidden. This aspect of his role is crucial to maintaining the sanctity of divine wisdom. It ensures that spiritual growth remains a genuine quest and not a mere acquisition of information. This balance between revelation and mystery preserves the integrity and depth of spiritual exploration, making it a truly transformative process.

In the wider context of the cosmic order, Metatron's role as Guardian of Knowledge positions him as a key architect of divine strategy, ensuring that the flow of spiritual wisdom conforms to the divine plan.

His actions and decisions are aligned with the greater purposes of the Universe, supporting the unfolding of cosmic events in a manner that is beneficial to all of creation.

His influence is also felt in the way he inspires humanity to preserve and cherish its spiritual heritage. Through his example and guidance, he encourages the creation of libraries, universities and other institutions dedicated to the pursuit of knowledge. These institutions serve as earthly mirrors of his heavenly library, acting as centres of learning where people can access and interact with the wealth of human understanding and divine wisdom.

Finally, his legacy as Guardian of Knowledge is one of empowerment. By making divine wisdom accessible to humanity, he empowers people to take control of their spiritual destiny. This empowerment refers not only to personal enlightenment, but also to contributing to the collective wisdom of humanity, thereby influencing societies and cultures in a profound and positive way.

Thus we are reminded of the depth and breadth of his duties and the profound impact he has on those who seek to understand the mysteries of life and the universe. Metatron is not only the guardian of divine secrets, but also a guide and mentor, guiding us through the complexities of our spiritual journeys towards a greater understanding of our place in the cosmos.

Chapter Four
The Midwayer

In the pantheon of celestial beings, Metatron occupies a unique position as the mediator between the divine and the mundane. His unique ability to act as a bridge between the two worlds is fundamental to the flow of communication and grace between Heaven and Earth.

Because of his unparalleled closeness to the Creator, Metatron is often referred to as the "Angel of the Covenant", a title that reflects his function of maintaining and transmitting the divine covenants to humanity. He is the executor of heavenly decrees, charged with delivering important divine messages and overseeing the fulfilment of sacred laws by both angels and humans.

One of the most emblematic stories of his role as mediator is his involvement in the giving of the Torah to the people of Israel. Metatron not only facilitated the communication of divine laws, but also helped to interpret them for human beings, ensuring that God's wisdom and intentions were clearly understood and followed. This interaction is not only a testament to his spiritual importance, but also a demonstration of his deep compassion and commitment to human welfare.

In addition to his role in transmitting laws and commandments, the Archangel also serves as a counsellor and guide for those seeking divine wisdom. He is accessible to mystics, sages and all those who sincerely seek a deeper connection with the Divine. His answers, often enigmatic and profound, are designed to stimulate reflection and spiritual growth, challenging people to explore beyond the surface of their spiritual practices.

He is also known for his ability to mediate conflicts, both celestial and earthly. In times of turmoil and disagreement, he is called upon to restore harmony and facilitate communication between conflicting parties. His deep understanding of divine motivations and laws makes him an effective mediator, able to find fair and just solutions that reflect the Creator's will.

Their role as mediators is particularly important in times of transition and change. Whether guiding souls through death to the afterlife or helping the living through moments of spiritual crisis, he offers support and guidance. This ability to act at thresholds, at points of critical transition, is one of the reasons why he is so revered and respected in different spiritual traditions.

When we consider the breadth of his role as The Go-Between, it becomes clear that Metatron is more than a messenger or guardian; he is a vital element of the spiritual infrastructure that sustains the universe. His presence and actions are essential in maintaining order, justice and communication between all aspects of creation, facilitating a continuous flow of grace and wisdom through the realms.

His ability to navigate between the divine and the human is not only a function of his exalted position, but also a reflection of his intimate understanding of both human and divine needs. This duality in his role allows him to adapt celestial messages to be understandable and relevant to humans, while remaining true to the divine essence.

Metatron often appears at times of important revelation, serving as a channel through which spiritual knowledge is transmitted to the world. One such occasion is during moments of great spiritual and artistic inspiration, when he is perceived as the motivating force behind creative insights that have profound spiritual and cultural implications. His presence in these circumstances emphasises the belief that the Divine communicates with humanity through a variety of means, including the arts.

In the context of mediation and intercession, the archangel is not limited to delivering messages. He is also invoked in healing rituals and purification ceremonies, where he acts as a channel for divine grace. In these rituals, he is usually called upon to help clear rooms of negative energy, heal spiritual wounds or even guide lost souls towards the light. His ability to purify and sanctify is an important aspect of his role as a mediator, demonstrating his function as a purifier and renewer of the human spirit.

He also plays a crucial role in protecting divine truths from being misinterpreted or manipulated. In an age when information can be distorted or lost, Metatron's function as guardian of the divine word is more important than ever. He ensures that the sacred teachings are preserved in their purest form and are accessible to those who sincerely seek the truth.

Metatron also helps to facilitate interfaith dialogue and mutual understanding between different spiritual traditions. He is seen as an ambassador of the divine, transcending sectarian barriers and promoting peace and understanding between different religious communities. This role is particularly important in a world where religious differences often lead to conflict and misunderstanding.

His presence in such interactions is a reminder that at the heart of all religious and spiritual traditions is a common quest to understand the divine. He not only communicates this universal truth, but also helps to create a space where this truth can be explored and celebrated together, regardless of cultural or spiritual differences.

As a mediator, Metatron is therefore a figure of immense importance and ability, whose actions continue to shape human spiritual experience in countless ways. His ability to facilitate communication between heaven and earth is not simply a matter of passing on messages; it is an essential function that underpins universal harmony and spiritual understanding.

His role as mediator extends into the realm of cosmic justice and balance, where he acts as an intermediary between the laws of the universe and the actions of heavenly and earthly beings. This complex responsibility involves not only enforcing divine decrees, but also ensuring that mercy and justice are balanced in every judgement.

One of the main aspects of Metatron's mediating role is his involvement in the judgement of souls. He is often imagined at the head of the celestial court, where the deeds of souls are compared with divine law. Metatron's presence in these settings emphasises his role as a compassionate judge who not only upholds the law, but also understands the complexities of human nature and the challenges faced by souls on their earthly journey.

Metatron's ability to navigate between strict justice and compassionate mercy is a testament to his deep understanding of the divine will and the human condition. This balance is fundamental, ensuring that divine laws are respected while mercy is extended to those who genuinely seek redemption and transformation. This dual capacity makes Metatron a fundamental figure in the spiritual development of souls, guiding them towards enlightenment and reconciliation with the Divine.

Metatron's work as a mediator also involves the management of the spiritual energies that flow between heaven and earth. He regulates these energies to ensure that they are in harmony with the spiritual readiness of the world and its inhabitants. This regulation helps to maintain a balance that prevents the spiritual energies from becoming overwhelming or misaligned with humanity's stage of development.

Metatron's guidance is particularly sought in times of spiritual turmoil, or when the human world faces significant challenges that have a spiritual basis. At such times he can channel higher energies to stabilise the spiritual atmosphere and support those working for peace and healing. His interventions can be subtle or profound, depending on the needs of the moment and the divine directives he receives.

Metatron also plays a vital role in the spiritual education of humanity. He imparts esoteric knowledge to selected individuals who are destined to assist in the spiritual evolution of their fellow human beings. This knowledge is usually advanced and complex, and requires a mediator of Metatron's calibre to ensure that it is properly understood and applied.

His teachings generally go beyond the boundaries of traditional spiritual paths, offering new insights and methods of connecting with the Divine. These teachings not only broaden the spiritual horizons of those who receive them, but also contribute to an overall increase in global spiritual awareness. Through this educational role, Metatron actively participates in the spiritual awakening of the planet, promoting a deeper collective understanding of the divine principles that govern the universe.

In short, the Archangel's function as a mediator is the cornerstone of his celestial duties. Through their efforts, the bridge between the divine and the human is not only maintained but strengthened, facilitating a deeper and more harmonious interaction between the two realms. His work ensures that divine guidance and justice are accessible to all beings, providing a basis for spiritual growth and cosmic harmony.

Metatron's role as a mediator is essential not only in the celestial spheres, but also in directly assisting individuals on their spiritual journeys on earth. He is particularly revered for his ability to offer personalised and profound guidance to those seeking spiritual growth, working in such a way that each piece of advice or insight is perfectly tailored to the needs of each soul.

In many spiritual traditions, he is known for his ability to open the 'eyes of the heart', allowing individuals to see beyond the illusions of the material world and perceive the deeper truths that govern our existence. This process of opening is essential for spiritual awakening and is usually accompanied by experiences of enlightenment that transform the lives of those involved.

Metatron's role in facilitating these experiences is multifaceted. He not only introduces new spiritual concepts and perspectives, but also helps to remove the blocks that prevent people from reaching a higher understanding. Through his intervention, psychic and emotional barriers are often overcome, allowing greater harmony and understanding to flow into the lives of those who seek his guidance.

As well as working as a personal guide, Metatron is often called upon to act in situations of global crisis or in challenges that affect large groups of people. In these cases his ability to mediate spiritual energies becomes crucial. He helps to co-ordinate the celestial responses to these situations, ensuring that divine interventions are carried out effectively and in harmony with the greater good of all concerned.

Metatron also plays a fundamental role in maintaining the connections between the different levels of reality. He helps to establish and maintain energy channels between the physical world and the spiritual realms, facilitating a continuous flow of spiritual energy essential for the sustenance of the planet and its inhabitants. This regulation of energy not only supports environmental and spiritual stability, but also promotes peace and general well-being.

Metatron is often seen as a catalyst for spiritual renewal and rebirth. He helps people to release old, outdated patterns that no longer serve their highest good, and encourages them to adopt new practices and ideas that are in line with their spiritual evolution. This process of transformation is essential for individual and collective growth, allowing a greater expression of human potential.

It also has a special role in protecting those at the forefront of spiritual and philosophical thought. Those who bring new ideas and perspectives to their communities often face resistance or misunderstanding. Metatron offers support to these pioneers, giving them clarity and the strength to continue their work despite the challenges.

In situations of conflict or confusion, Metatron's ability to mediate and bring clarity is most evident. Not only does he help to resolve disagreements, but he also works to ensure that solutions are reached in a fair and balanced way, respecting the needs of all parties involved. This aspect of his work is vital in promoting peace and harmony on both a small and large scale.

Metatron is also known for his ability to connect people and ideas from different walks of life, facilitating a broader and more inclusive dialogue on spiritual and worldly issues. He encourages cooperation between different cultures and spiritual traditions, helping to create a common ground on which mutual understanding can flourish. This ability to unite diverse groups is a fundamental aspect of his role as a mediator, as it strengthens the network of human and spiritual connections around the world.

It is clear that Metatron's influence is immeasurable and multi-dimensional. He not only communicates the divine will, but also facilitates the practical application of that will in people's daily lives. Metatron continues to be a source of wisdom and guidance for all who seek truth and understanding in an ever-changing world. With his help we can navigate the complexities of existence with greater confidence and clarity, moving towards a future where harmony between heaven and earth can be fully realised.

Chapter Five
Attributed Miracles

As well as being an archangel associated with wisdom and mediation, Metatron is also recognised for his ability to perform miracles. These miraculous acts, often manifested in times of great need, serve as testimony to divine power and heavenly intercession in the lives of the faithful.

One of the most famous miracles associated with Metatron took place at a time of great unrest and danger for a group of believers. According to reports, a community was about to be devastated by an impending natural disaster. In an act of desperate faith, the leaders of the community called upon Metatron to protect them. The chronicles of this event describe how a storm inexplicably changed course and spared the community from destruction. Many have attributed this direct miracle to the intervention of Metatron, who is said to have acted as a shield against the forces of nature.

Another example of Metatron's miraculous ability is the healing of diseases that were thought to be incurable. There are countless testimonies of people who, when all medical hope had been exhausted, turned to Metatron's intercession through prayer and ritual. Many of these people have reported miraculous recoveries that doctors and scientists have been unable to explain. These stories of healing reinforce the belief in the angel's power not only as a messenger of the divine, but also as an agent of renewal and hope.

Miracles of protection and spiritual guidance are also attributed to Metatron. On several occasions, people facing difficult decisions or at critical crossroads in their lives have reported feeling the angel's reassuring presence, guiding them towards choices that ultimately led to positive and transformative outcomes. These moments of guidance are seen as miraculous interventions that have helped to change the course of people's lives for the better.

It is also often associated with unexplained phenomena that occur during deep spiritual practices or moments of great religious celebration. Reports of visions, mystical lights, and sensations of warmth and unusual energy during prayer or meditation are common in texts documenting encounters with the angel. These events are interpreted as physical manifestations of Metatron's power, designed to strengthen faith and promote a deeper connection with the divine.

These miracles attributed to Metatron not only reinforce his position as a powerful archangel, but also serve as points of connection between heaven and earth, tangibly demonstrating the divine's ongoing concern for the well-being of humanity. Each miracle is a reminder of divine love and mercy, and of Metatron's special role in facilitating that grace.

Metatron's miracles include not only crisis intervention and healing, but also spiritual protection and enlightenment. He is often invoked to protect against negative energies and to purify places and people, restoring harmony and peace to environments disturbed by evil influences.

One remarkable account of Metatron's ability to provide spiritual protection occurred at a sacred site that was threatened with desecration. According to the believers, when the situation seemed irreversible, Metatron's fervent invocation resulted in a series of inexplicable events that drove away the aggressors and preserved the sanctity of the site. This intervention not only saved the physical space, but also reinforced the people's belief in the angel's active and caring presence in the defence of sacred spaces.

Metatron is also known for his miracles of spiritual enlightenment, especially in contexts where people or groups seek to understand deep spiritual mysteries or to reach elevated states of consciousness. There are several accounts of him guiding meditators and seekers through visions and revelations that have profoundly expanded their spiritual understanding and connection. These experiences often lead to significant personal transformations and a new understanding of the nature of the universe and humanity's role within it.

A particularly impressive example of this form of miracle involved an academic who was struggling with deep doubts about his faith. After seeking Metatron's intercession, he had a series of vivid dreams in which the Archangel showed him the interconnectedness of all forms of life and the presence of the Divine in every part of creation. These visions restored his faith and gave him a new sense of purpose, reinvigorating his spiritual practice and commitment to his religious path.

In addition to these more visible aspects, Metatron's miracles also include facilitating communication between the living and the dead. In various cultures, Metatron is seen as a guide for souls in transition to the afterlife, ensuring that they don't get lost and reach their destination. For those who remain, these stories provide comfort and confirmation that life continues beyond physical existence and that there are celestial beings watching over the souls' journey.

Each of these miracles attributed to Metatron not only reinforces his stature as a powerful celestial mediator, but also highlights his accessibility and willingness to intervene on behalf of humanity. They are tangible manifestations of his mercy and power, testifying to his continuing commitment to helping humanity in its quest for protection, healing and spiritual enlightenment.

Metatron's ability to perform miracles is not limited to large-scale events; he is also known to intervene in personal situations, touching people's lives in deeply personal and meaningful ways. These interventions, usually subtle, are just as powerful as the most spectacular because they change a person's life in a direct and lasting way.

One striking example of a personal miracle involves an individual who was facing a long period of despair and loss of meaning in life. After many unsuccessful attempts to find comfort and understanding through conventional means, the individual turned to Metatron in prayer. In response, the angel manifested in a dream, offering words of comfort and a symbolic vision that restored hope and direction to the individual's life. The message received in this encounter not only relieved the person's emotional suffering, but also gave them a new understanding of the divine plans and their own role in the world.

Metatron is also celebrated for his miracles of synchronicity, where circumstances seem to align perfectly to meet the needs or solve the problems of individuals in unexpected ways. Often described as small miracles, these events reinforce the idea that the angel is constantly present, guiding and adjusting the course of events to reflect a greater plan. Whether it's helping someone find a lost object of great personal significance, or facilitating a chance encounter that leads to a life-changing opportunity, these acts of synchronicity are powerful reminders of Metatron's ongoing care.

In addition to these direct interventions, miracles usually involve the empowerment of people to carry out their own transformations. The angel is known for awakening latent spiritual abilities in people, allowing them to access deeper levels of consciousness and healing abilities. This empowerment not only changes the life of the individual, but also has a ripple effect, benefiting others around them through their new gifts and abilities.

Another aspect of Metatron's miracles is his ability to protect against imminent danger. There are accounts of people who have inexplicably deviated from a course of action that would have led to tragedy, and many attribute this sudden change of plans to the angel's discreet influence. This protection is often seen as an unseen blessing, a guardian force that intervenes to preserve the lives and well-being of those under its care.

When we consider the range of miracles attributed to Metatron, it becomes clear that his work as a mediator goes beyond simply delivering divine messages or performing impressive feats. He touches lives in a deeply personal and transformative way, acting as a true guardian, guide and mentor to those who seek his help. Whether in times of critical need or in everyday matters, the angel remains a symbol of hope and divine intervention, always ready to offer support and guidance.

Among the many miracles attributed to Metatron, some of the most notable relate to his ability to inspire social and spiritual change on a large scale. Metatron not only works on an individual level, but also influences entire communities, bringing enlightenment and spiritual renewal to many at once.

A striking example of this ability occurred in a small town facing a collective crisis of faith, exacerbated by internal divisions and community conflicts. The situation seemed hopeless until the community turned to Metatron for intercession. In response, the angel manifested himself in such a way that all the inhabitants of the town shared the same profound vision during a local religious event. This shared experience acted as a catalyst for reconciliation and spiritual renewal, uniting the community and restoring their collective faith and purpose.

As well as inspiring spiritual renewal, Metatron is also revered for his ability to protect against natural and human disasters. There are stories of villages miraculously spared from natural disasters after their inhabitants prayed to Metatron, as in the example quoted earlier. These stories are usually accompanied by reports of unexplained phenomena, such as sudden changes in the weather or the direction of forest fires, which are seen as signs of divine intervention.

Metatron is also known for performing miracles of reconciliation and peace between peoples and nations in conflict. His role as mediator is crucial in delicate diplomatic situations, where he is invoked to soften hardened hearts and pave the way for peaceful negotiations. On several historical occasions, the interventions attributed to Metatron have helped to prevent wars and promote peace agreements, reinforcing his reputation as an archangel of great power and compassion.

Metatron's miracles also extend to the realm of creation and innovation. He is seen as the patron of inventors and thinkers, inspiring them to develop technologies and ideas that benefit humanity in significant ways. Many important innovations, especially those that promote health and well-being, are attributed to the divine inspiration received through his influence.

These examples illustrate the breadth and depth of Metatron's impact on the world. His miracles are not just one-off interventions; they are transformations that have a lasting and significant reach. Each of the angel's miracles strengthens the fabric of society, promoting not only the survival but the spiritual and material flourishing of communities around the world.

Metatron's influence and miracles are not confined to the spiritual or religious spheres; they permeate people's everyday lives, touching the practical aspects of life in often surprising and profound ways. Through his interventions he demonstrates that the divine is inextricably linked to all aspects of human experience.

A particularly moving aspect of Metatron's miracles is his ability to bring comfort and peace to people facing the end of their lives or dealing with the loss of loved ones. Many accounts describe how Metatron's presence in hospitals or nursing homes at the time of death has provided a peaceful and serene transition for both the dying and their families. It is believed that his influence helps to alleviate fear and pain, bringing a sense of acceptance and understanding of the natural cycle of life and death.

In addition, miracles often take the form of synchronicities that guide people to make choices that positively change the course of their lives. These are not random coincidences; they are carefully orchestrated moments that seem to conspire to bring about the best possible outcome. Whether it's helping someone find the right job at the right time, or guiding someone to reconnect with an old friend who can offer support at a crucial moment, Metatron is seen as the mentor behind these meaningful encounters.

He is also recognised for providing miracles that strengthen the connection between people and the natural environment. On several occasions, communities facing environmental challenges such as drought or pollution have seen significant improvements after calling on his help. These interventions are seen as a reminder that caring for our planet is a shared responsibility between humanity and the divine, with the angel acting as a facilitator of this sacred partnership.

The miracles attributed to him teach us that the Archangel doesn't just respond to requests for help; he anticipates the needs of those under his care. His commitment to facilitating well-being and spiritual evolution is a testament to his unwavering devotion and the divine love he represents. Every miracle, large or small, is a manifestation of his active presence and his desire to see all beings live in harmony and peace.

Metatron's miracles make it clear that his role as a celestial mediator is not only a position of power and authority, but also one of deep empathy and care. He is not distant; he is deeply involved in the struggles and joys of human life, offering his strength and guidance to transform the ordinary into the extraordinary.

Chapter Six
The Cult of Metatron

The cult of Metatron, although not as widely recognised as that of other archangels, is embedded in traditions and practices that span different cultures and eras. The worship of Metatron generally takes place in esoteric and mystical contexts, where he is seen as a powerful intercessor and spiritual guide.

Among followers of the Kabbalah, Metatron is considered one of the highest archangels, especially associated with the Sefirah Kether, which represents the crown and highest point of the Tree of Life. His closeness to God makes him a central figure in meditation and other practices that seek spiritual ascension and an understanding of celestial structures.

One of the most common forms of Metatron worship involves meditation and the recitation of mantras or prayers believed to attract his presence and help. These practices are not simply invocation rituals; they are seen as a means of aligning the practitioner's soul with higher energies, facilitating a direct connection with the angel. Practitioners often report experiences of profound revelation and feelings of peace during these practices, reinforcing their belief in the efficacy of their devotion.

In addition to meditative practices, many devotees wear amulets and talismans that are believed to be blessed with their protection. These objects are usually inscribed with symbols and holy names associated with Metatron and are used to attract health, prosperity and spiritual protection. The use of these amulets is particularly popular among those who engage in activities considered spiritually risky, such as the study and practice of ceremonial magic or intense spirituality.

Celebrations in honour of Metatron usually coincide with dates that have astronomical or numerological significance, reflecting his connection with the fundamental structures of the universe. During these events, rituals are performed that celebrate his wisdom and power, and participants seek his blessing for new beginnings or the renewal of their spiritual commitments. These celebrations may include music, dance, offerings and extended meditations, all designed to honour Metatron and integrate his energies into the lives of the practitioners.

The influence of Metatron's cult is also evident in the role he plays as a model of spiritual service. His followers often see themselves as part of a tradition that not only seeks personal growth, but also contributes to the collective good. Through Metatron's example, they are encouraged to use their own spiritual gifts to help others by spreading his healing and protective energies through actions in the material world.

The traditions surrounding the cult of Metatron are as diverse as the cultures that adopt them, reflecting a variety of interpretations and practices dedicated to this powerful archangel. These traditions not only illustrate worship, but also provide insights into how different communities understand and interact with the divine through his figure.

In some traditions, Metatron is seen as the guardian of sacred scriptures and divine secrets, making him a focal point in rituals that seek to reveal occult or mystical knowledge. In these contexts, rituals dedicated to Metatron usually involve complex initiation ceremonies in which participants go through various stages of purification and enlightenment with the aim of getting closer to the sacred knowledge that Metatron protects.

Another important aspect of the Metatron cult is his representation in art and literature. He is often depicted in iconography and religious texts as a celestial warrior or a divine sage, each representation highlighting different aspects of his character and service. These representations are not merely ornamental; they serve as a focus of meditation for devotees, helping them to visualise and invoke the angel's presence in their spiritual practices.

In addition, the cult of Metatron involves the formation of religious communities that come together to study his teachings and celebrate his influence on their lives. These communities, often transnational and linked by modern networks, share resources, insights and support, strengthening their collective devotion and their particular understanding of Metatron. Within these communities, the angel is often invoked in collective prayers and group practices aimed not only at worship, but also at mutual support and spiritual growth.

Festivals and holy days dedicated to Metatron are special moments of celebration and reverence. During these times, devotees engage in a variety of activities, from fasts and vigils to feasts and community services, each reflecting different aspects of their faith and worship. These events are also opportunities to teach new generations about Metatron, ensuring that knowledge and respect for this archangel continues to flourish.

Another facet of Metatron's cult is the practice of pilgrimage to places considered sacred to Metatron. These are usually the sites of past miraculous manifestations or places where Metatron is said to have given visions or revelations. These pilgrimages are not only spiritual journeys, but also opportunities for devotees to connect more deeply with the angel, seeking his guidance and blessings in a more immersive and concentrated way.

The cult of Metatron, with its diversity of forms and expressions, demonstrates the depth and complexity of his figure as a mediator between the divine and the human. He serves not only as a point of access to the divine, but also as a catalyst for spiritual and communal expression, significantly influencing the lives of his followers.

The depth of devotion can be seen not only in everyday practices and celebrations, but also in the way it influences art, literature and theological thought. These cultural manifestations offer a broader view of how the Angel is perceived and worshipped in different spiritual and religious traditions.

In mystical literature, especially in the context of the Kabbalah and other esoteric texts, Metatron is often described as the "Angel of the Presence", a being who embodies the immanence of God. These texts explore his complex interactions with the Divine and with humanity, presenting him as a key to unlocking the mysteries of existence. Scholars and mystics who delve into these writings often find them a rich source of symbolism and spiritual teachings that guide their own journeys of faith.

Religious art also plays a fundamental role in spreading the cult of Metatron. He is often depicted in icons, paintings and sculptures used in places of worship and in private spaces as a focus for meditation and devotion. These artistic representations not only embellish sacred spaces, but also serve as visual reminders of the archangel's power and presence. Art becomes a portal through which devotees can connect with the angel for inspiration and comfort.

The cult has also influenced music and sacred hymns in various traditions. Music dedicated to Metatron or invoking his presence is used in liturgies and devotional practices, where it serves as a means of uplifting the soul and facilitating a deeper spiritual experience. These hymns and songs strengthen the community of faith by uniting believers in a common expression of reverence and worship.

The influence of Metatron's cult is also evident in religious and spiritual education, where he is often presented as an example of worship and spiritual commitment. Teachers and spiritual leaders use his figure to teach the values of obedience, wisdom and compassion, and to inspire believers to follow a path of integrity and service.

Community practices around the cult of Metatron often include acts of charity and community service, in which followers are encouraged to manifest divine love and mercy in the material world. These activities not only benefit local communities, but also reinforce the spiritual principles that Metatron represents, transforming devotion into concrete actions that reflect the devotee's commitment to his ideals. The cult of Metatron is therefore a vibrant and diverse expression of human spirituality. Not only does it serve as a bridge between the divine and the mundane, but it also inspires a rich tradition of art, music, literature and community action that enriches the spiritual lives of its followers around the world.

The cult is also deeply rooted in personal practices that reflect an intimate relationship between the devotee and the divine. Many followers of Metatron cultivate daily practices that not only honour the archangel, but also seek to integrate his attributes and teachings into their own lives.

For devotees of Metatron, starting the day with a prayer or meditation focused on his figure is a way of ensuring protection and spiritual guidance. These morning practices are considered essential for aligning the day's energy with the qualities of wisdom and clarity associated with the angel. Many report that this moment of connection helps to establish a firm foundation for the challenges of daily life, and reminds them of their constant connection with the Divine.

The study of sacred texts associated with Metatron is another central practice for those who follow the archangel. Taking the time to read and contemplate these writings allows devotees to deepen their understanding of spiritual mysteries and strengthen their connection. This practice is usually accompanied by study groups and community discussions, where devotees share insights and inspirations from their readings and personal experiences.

Rituals dedicated to Metatron usually include offerings of incense, candles and other items thought to be pleasing to the archangel. These offerings are a way of showing respect and gratitude for his constant protection and guidance. In addition, these rituals may include chanting, the recitation of mantras and the recitation of specific prayers to invoke his presence and blessings.

Although the cult of Metatron can be a personal journey, it also has a strong communal component. Many Metatron worshipping communities organise regular events and celebrations that bring believers together to pay homage to the archangel. These celebrations are opportunities to strengthen community bonds, share spiritual experiences, and renew collective commitment to the paths taught by the Archangel.

In addition to these more formalised practices, followers of Metatron often look for ways to integrate the Archangel's teachings and essence into their daily lives. This may involve practising acts of kindness and mercy, seeking to bring harmony where there is discord, and seeking justice where there is injustice. These daily actions reflect the practical and transformative impact of worship on the lives of individuals and their communities.

Through these diverse practices, worship transcends the spectrum of simple veneration; it becomes a way of life, a way of navigating the world with a higher consciousness and a clear spiritual purpose. As a model of wisdom and divine mediation, Metatron continues to inspire and guide his followers in their ongoing quest for a more fulfilling and spiritually integrated life.

In addition to individual and communal practices, the cult is characterised by a deep reverence for his ability to intercede in matters of great spiritual and material importance. Devotees generally regard the Archangel as an essential guide on their spiritual journey, and seek his help at times of significant decision and change.

One of the most valued facets of Metatron in his cult is his role as an intercessor. Followers believe that he has the ability to present their prayers directly to God, acting as a messenger of their requests and desires. This belief strengthens followers' trust in his protection and guidance, especially in times of uncertainty or difficulty. His intercession is often sought in prayers for healing, conflict resolution and protection from harm.

Metatron is also associated with rituals of purification and spiritual renewal. Because of his exalted position as an almost divine being, he has the power to cleanse negative energy and restore spiritual order. Followers can take part in purification baths, cleansing meditations and other practices that involve invoking Metatron to rejuvenate and revitalise their spiritual lives.

The cult of Metatron also includes the observance of certain holy days and festivals dedicated to him. These occasions are moments of communal celebration, spiritual reflection and renewal of commitment to his teachings. During these festivals, stories are shared, lessons are reviewed and the community gathers to honour their celestial leader with music, dance and offerings.

In addition to devotional practices, the cult of Metatron usually involves education and the dissemination of his teachings. This may include formal study in esoteric schools, workshops and seminars, or even the publication of books and other materials exploring aspects of his nature and work. Through these educational efforts, the knowledge is kept alive and accessible to new generations of devotees.

The practice of passing on the knowledge and worship of Metatron not only enriches the spiritual lives of individuals, but also strengthens the faith community as a whole. It creates a network of support and a rich spiritual tradition that continues to inspire and guide people around the world.

The cult of Metatron is a testament to this archangel's enduring influence on diverse cultures and spiritual traditions. His devotional practices, teachings and rituals continue to offer guidance, comfort and inspiration to those seeking a deeper connection with the divine. Metatron remains a central figure in the spiritual journey of many, a guardian of celestial wisdom and a powerful intercessor on the celestial plane.

Chapter Seven
Spiritual Practices

As well as being an archangel of great miracles and intercession, Metatron is also a central figure in various spiritual practices that seek to raise consciousness and deepen connection with the Divine.

One of the most common practices associated with him is meditation, especially those involving visualisation and the channeling of celestial energies. Metatron is often invoked as a guide during deep meditations, especially those that seek to access higher levels of consciousness or explore deeper spiritual dimensions. Devotees believe that with his help they can reach states of consciousness that provide clarity, inner peace and spiritual insight.

Metatron is also known as a powerful spiritual protector. Many practices involve invoking him to protect the individual from negative energies or harmful influences. This is usually done through prayers, incantations or the creation of protective circles energised by his presence. These protective practices are particularly valued by those involved in spiritual or paranormal work, where protection from destabilising forces is crucial.

As the guardian of heavenly knowledge, many spiritual practices revolve around the study of scripture and sacred texts. Followers typically devote themselves to the intensive study of texts believed to have been influenced or transmitted by the Archangel. These studies may involve the exploration of complex issues such as the nature of the soul, the purpose of life and the structure of the cosmos, all seen through the lens of the teachings transmitted by the Archangel.

He is often associated with spiritual healing practices, as it is believed that he can facilitate the healing of not only physical ailments, but also emotional and spiritual wounds.

Healing techniques may include the laying on of hands, healing prayers and the use of sacred symbols that carry Metatron's healing energy. These practices are usually accompanied by a deep sense of renewal and well-being.

He also plays an important role in transitional rituals, such as those that mark important passages in life, including births, weddings and even death. In these rituals, the archangel is called upon to bless those involved and to ensure that the transition takes place in a harmonious and protected manner. These rituals highlight Metatron's role as a guide through the different stages of life, offering support and protection at times of significant change.

These spiritual practices reflect his versatility as an archangel, facilitating personal and community growth on many levels. Each practice is an opportunity for people to connect more deeply with the Divine and to experience Metatron's guidance and love in their lives.

The Archangel is often associated with cleansing and consecration rituals, which are essential for maintaining the purity of sacred spaces and individuals. These rituals involve the use of elements such as water, incense and specific prayers that invoke him to cleanse and consecrate places of worship, religious objects or even people. These practices are particularly important before significant spiritual events to ensure that all participants and the environment are free of negative influences and ready to receive divine blessings.

As well as guiding meditations for protection and healing, Metatron is seen as an important facilitator on the journey of spiritual ascension. He is seen as a bridge between the physical world and the higher spiritual realms. Meditation guides who invoke him usually focus on ascending through the chakras, seeking to purify and align these energy centres to facilitate a deeper spiritual awakening. These practices are designed to help practitioners transcend earthly limitations and access higher states of consciousness.

The Archangel's wisdom is also shared through formal teachings and workshops that address various aspects of his energy and how to work with it. These educational events are opportunities to deepen your knowledge of Metatron, learn specific techniques for invoking his presence, and better understand his influence in various areas of life. Spiritual teachers who specialise in Metatron's energy offer insights into how to integrate his qualities into daily life practices and spirituality.

Metatron is also known for his ability to communicate through mediums and channelers. Channeling practices involving him can include direct messages from this archangel offering guidance, comfort and predictions for the future. These channeling sessions are powerful moments of spiritual communication where participants can feel a direct connection to the Divine through the words and energy of the Archangel.

Working with Metatron can involve the development of intuition and spiritual perception. Devotees and spiritual practitioners often seek his help to enhance their psychic and spiritual abilities, enabling them to perceive the subtleties of the spiritual world with greater clarity and precision. These abilities are crucial for those involved in advanced spiritual practices and can be greatly enhanced through his guidance.

These diverse spiritual practices not only illustrate Metatron's multi-functionality as a spiritual guide and protector, but also highlight his accessibility to those seeking depth and authenticity in their spiritual journey. Through these practices, the Archangel continues to inspire, heal and uplift those who invoke him, enriching their lives with celestial wisdom and divine love.

Metatron is often associated with nature and the elements, and is invoked in ceremonies that seek to harmonise human beings with the natural environment. These ceremonies may include walks in sacred places, outdoor rituals using natural elements such as water, stones and plants, and meditations focused on the energy of the earth. Followers believe that the archangel helps to strengthen this connection with the natural world, which is essential for spiritual and physical health.

Another important facet of related spiritual practices is the release and healing of ancestors. Many followers turn to him to resolve problems or traumas that have been passed down from generation to generation. Through healing rituals, guided meditations and prayers, Metatron is called upon to help release these ancestral patterns and promote the healing not only of the individual, but of the entire family lineage. This practice is seen as vital for releasing emotional and spiritual burdens that can affect present life.

Metatron is also revered for his ability to guide the faithful through vision journeys and lucid dreams.

Advanced practitioners who work with him often report experiences in which he appears in their dreams or meditations, offering guidance, revealing profound messages or taking them to other dimensions. These experiences are considered highly transformative, capable of changing a person's perception of reality and their purpose in life.

In addition to practices that focus on protection and enlightenment, the cult emphasises the development of compassion and universal wisdom. Followers are encouraged to incorporate these qualities into their daily lives, seeking to live in a way that reflects the principles of unconditional love and deep understanding that Metatron exemplifies. This may involve random acts of kindness, volunteering or simply approaching everyday situations with a more centred and aware attitude.

Many devotees participate in spiritual retreats dedicated to the Archangel, where they spend days or even weeks immersed in practices that honour and invoke his presence. These retreats offer an opportunity to get away from the distractions of the modern world and deepen one's spiritual connection through intense prayer, study, meditation and fellowship with other devotees.

These spiritual practices show how Metatron is perceived and revered as a powerful and versatile guide, capable of profoundly influencing the spiritual journey of his followers. Through these practices, devotees seek not only personal growth, but also greater harmony with the universe and a deeper understanding of the divine mysteries.

The archangel is also often associated with occult knowledge and divination practices, and is seen as a master of divine mysteries who can reveal hidden secrets and offer clarity about the future. Devotees and practitioners of the mystical arts use various forms of divination, such as tarot, astrology and numerology, invoking Metatron to guide their interpretations and decisions. It is believed that his presence increases the accuracy and depth of the readings and connects the practitioner to a divine source of wisdom.

Metatron is also invoked in rituals of personal transformation in which participants seek to change significant aspects of their lives. These rituals may involve overcoming addictions, changing harmful behaviours, or developing new skills and talents. The archangel is seen as a catalyst for change, providing the energy and support needed for people to realise their aspirations and improve their lives.

Maintaining energy balance is another area where the practices associated with Metatron are particularly valued. He is considered an expert in harmonising energy fields, balancing the chakras and cleansing the aura. Practices such as crystal placement, the use of aromatherapy and Reiki sessions often include invocations to Metatron to enhance the effects of these techniques and promote a state of well-being and inner harmony.

It is also celebrated in synchrony with important cosmic cycles such as equinoxes, solstices and planetary alignments. During these times, special ceremonies and meditations are held to honour Metatron's influence on the cosmic order and to seek his guidance in understanding the energies at play. These celebrations are seen as powerful moments of spiritual connection and personal recalibration, aligning participants with the greater forces of the universe.

Worship often leads to the development of spiritual communities in which teachings and practices are shared and lived together. These communities not only offer mutual support and guidance, but also serve as spaces for spiritual growth and transformation. Through community, Metatron's teachings are disseminated more widely, reaching more lives and increasing the impact of his spiritual practices.

The spiritual practices associated with Metatron are diverse and deeply enriching, offering multiple paths for those seeking to deepen their understanding and connection with the Divine. Through these practices, Metatron continues to be a source of inspiration and guidance for many, helping them to face life's challenges with greater wisdom and balance.

A fundamental associated spiritual practice is the creation and maintenance of sacred spaces. These places are dedicated to meditation, prayer and rituals that invoke the Archangel's presence for protection and enlightenment. Sacred spaces can range from small altars in homes to large temples in communities. Devotees believe that these spaces strengthen the connection, facilitate a continuous flow of divine energy and promote an environment of peace and spirituality.

Metatron is honoured on various commemorative dates that have special meanings based on ancient traditions or modern revelations. During these festivals, ceremonies are held that may include dances, music, offerings and purification rituals. These events serve not only to reaffirm the faith of the participants, but also to invigorate the community with their sacred energy, creating moments of unity and collective celebration.

The use of daily prayers and specific mantras is a common practice among his followers. These prayers are often recited at the beginning and end of the day and are used to ask for guidance, protection and wisdom. The mantras, in turn, are used to align the mind and spirit with Metatron's qualities, helping practitioners to focus on their spiritual goals and live according to divine principles.

Dedicated spiritual retreats offer devotees the opportunity to step away from the distractions of everyday life and delve deeper into their spiritual practice. At these retreats, participants take part in a range of activities such as workshops, lectures, guided meditations and healing sessions, all designed to strengthen their connection with Metatron and explore new dimensions of their faith.

Many devotees are motivated to perform community service and acts of charity, seeing these actions as an extension of their spiritual practice. These acts are inspired by Metatron's teachings on compassion and service to others and are seen as a concrete way of manifesting his blessings in the material world.

The spiritual practices associated with Metatron are an expression of a deep commitment to spiritual growth and divine service. Through these practices, devotees not only seek their own enlightenment, but also contribute to the well-being of the world by spreading the virtues of wisdom, compassion and peace that Metatron exemplifies. Through their daily activities, rituals and celebrations, followers continue to bring his energy and sacred presence into the reality of their lives, creating an ongoing bridge between heaven and earth.

Chapter Eight
Metatron's Protection

In angelic spirituality and belief, Metatron stands out as a bastion of protection. Revered as the 'Angel of the Presence', his ability to offer protection to those who seek his help is as revered as his other celestial roles.

Metatron is often described as the great archangel whose energy transcends common understanding, positioned as a force of protection against evil and negativity. Many mystical and spiritual traditions teach that invoking his protection strengthens a person's spiritual defences, protecting them from evil influences and even driving away negative entities.

The practice of invoking Metatron's protection usually involves specific rituals or prayers. These rituals usually begin with the cleansing of the physical and spiritual space, using elements such as salt, holy water or incense, which are considered powerful purifiers. Specific prayers or mantras are then recited to attract Metatron's attention and allow his presence and power to fill the environment or life of the person seeking protection.

The teachings on protection attributed to him are not simply reactive mechanisms to ward off evil; they also emphasise the importance of prevention and maintaining a state of spiritual purity. The Archangel teaches that true protection begins with self-knowledge and self-discipline, and that aligning thoughts, words and actions with divine light is the best defence against darkness.

In the stories told by those who believe they have been protected by Metatron, we find a variety of experiences, from feeling a comforting presence in moments of fear to miraculous interventions in situations of imminent physical danger. These stories reinforce the belief in his ability to protect and serve as testimony to his vital role as a celestial guardian.

The effectiveness of Metatron's protection is generally linked to his ability to operate in several dimensions simultaneously, acting as a guardian who not only defends against perceived threats, but also strengthens a person's spiritual structure. This is achieved by deepening the spiritual connection, which helps the person to reach a higher state of consciousness in which negative vibrations have less impact.

A fundamental aspect of the associated protective practices is the use of symbols and sacred geometry. Metatron is often associated with the 'Metatron Cube', a geometric symbol that represents the energy field around the body and is used to cleanse and illuminate the spiritual environment. The cube is believed to act as a shield, filtering out negativity and impurities and maintaining a person's energetic integrity.

For devotees, the practice of visualising Metatron's Cube around the body is a powerful exercise. This is usually done during meditation, where the person imagines the cube spinning and its purifying energy dissolving any negativity or blockages that may be present. This visualisation not only strengthens personal protection, but also serves to raise the practitioner's spiritual vibration, bringing them closer to celestial frequencies.

Metatron is also invoked in situations that require protection beyond the individual, such as group events or projects that seek to promote collective peace and well-being. His presence is considered essential to ensure that the energies gathered are harmonised and directed towards constructive ends, avoiding interference or negative spiritual influences.

Metatron's protection also extends to places. Many spiritual traditions dedicate specific spaces for worship or invocation, creating sanctuaries where the archangel's protective energy can be felt at all times. These sacred spaces are often places of pilgrimage for those seeking spiritual refuge or to strengthen their faith and spiritual defences.

Invocations, especially those related to protection, are enriched with rituals that use physical and symbolic elements to reinforce the request for safety. These rituals usually involve the burning of incense or sacred herbs, the smoke of which carries the prayers of the faithful directly to Metatron. It is also common to use coloured candles, especially white or blue, which symbolise the purity and divine truth that the archangel represents.

These practices are usually accompanied by chanting or recitation of psalms and other sacred texts that mention protection. These texts are chosen for their high vibrations and their ability to connect the practitioner more directly with the celestial realm. By verbalising these sacred words, it is believed that the individual creates a stronger bond with Metatron, thus facilitating a more powerful response.

The archangel is also known for his ability to intercede in times of crisis or imminent danger. There are countless testimonies of people who, after invoking Metatron in a time of great need, experienced inexplicable and often miraculous changes that led them to safety. These experiences are often described as a feeling of a powerful, calming presence that provides mental clarity and tranquillity, allowing solutions to problems to emerge clearly.

In the context of spiritual protection, Metatron is seen as a mentor who teaches how people can strengthen their own spiritual barriers. Through his guidance, he shows how maintaining a clean and strong auric field not only repels negative influences, but also attracts positive forces. This spiritual education is fundamental as it allows people to take a more active role in maintaining their spiritual integrity.

The protection offered by Metatron transcends individual circumstances and extends to global efforts for peace and healing. In a world often troubled by conflict and disorder, his protective presence is invoked in rituals and ceremonies that seek to harmonise global energies and inspire reconciliation and mutual understanding between peoples.

In addition to individual protective practices, Metatron is often fundamental to celebrations and festivals that bring communities together to strengthen collective protection. These events are moments of great spiritual energy in which participants share not only rituals but also personal testimonies of Metatron's interventions in their lives, strengthening faith and connection with the community.

A common element of these meetings is the creation of altars or sacred spaces dedicated to the Archangel. These spaces are adorned with associated symbols, such as Metatron's cube and images or statues representing his figure. Participants bring offerings, which may include flowers, gems and scriptures considered to be of great spiritual significance, creating a vibrant atmosphere of worship and respect.

Guided meditations are often held at these gatherings, with the aim of connecting the participants directly with Metatron's energy. During these sessions, led by experienced spiritual leaders, participants are taken on visual journeys that explore spiritual protection in depth. These meditations are designed to leave a lasting impression and equip individuals with mental and spiritual tools that can be used in times of need.

In addition to the formal practices, teaching how to maintain a daily relationship with Metatron is an essential part of these meetings. Participants are encouraged to incorporate small rituals into their daily routines, such as saying small prayers when they wake up or before they go to sleep, in order to stay in constant contact. These practices help to create a sense of safety and security that permeates daily life.

These communities often share stories of how protection has manifested itself in their lives. Whether through happy coincidences that have averted disaster or moments of clarity that have led them to make safe decisions, these accounts reinforce belief in Metatron's power and inspire new members to seek his protection.

The celebration of Metatron as a protector testifies to the universality of the human desire for security and spiritual support. He is seen not only as a guardian against evil, but as a symbol of the constant presence of the divine in people's lives, a reminder that they are not alone in their struggles and that they can always seek refuge in his divine protection.

In addition to community gatherings and rituals, Metatron's protective influence extends into more personal and intimate spheres. People often recount experiences in which they have felt the archangel's direct intervention in moments of physical or spiritual danger, such as miraculously avoided accidents or surprising recoveries from serious illnesses. These personal experiences reinforce the belief in Metatron's power and role as a celestial protector.

The practice of wearing symbols, such as Metatron Cube pendants or amulets, is common among believers. It is believed that these objects act as energy conductors, providing an extra layer of protection against negative forces and promoting health and well-being. Wearers of these amulets often report a greater sense of security and calm, attributing these sensations to the archangel's presence and blessing.

Metatron is also regarded as the protector of children, and many parents invoke his protection for their children. It is taught that his presence protects young people from physical dangers and negative influences, while at the same time guiding their spiritual and moral growth. Prayers for the safety of children testify to his all-encompassing role as guardian of all who are vulnerable.

In the context of education and personal growth, Metatron is often called upon to guide and protect those on journeys of self-knowledge and spiritual transformation. He is seen as a guide who not only protects against deception and deviation, but also illuminates the path with wisdom and clarity, ensuring that learning is safe and fruitful.

Chapter Nine
Metatron and Healing

Among the many facets of the Archangel Metatron, his ability to facilitate spiritual and physical healing is one of the most revered; he assists in the process of restoring health, balancing energy and promoting general well-being.

Metatron is often associated with energy healing, particularly through the use of Sacred Geometry, which is said to contain patterns that resonate with the deepest structures of the universe. The Metatron Cube in particular is a powerful tool in this practice. It is used as a map or key to access and correct imbalances in the body's energy fields.

Metatron's work in the field of healing goes beyond simply adjusting energy. He is considered a master who imparts wisdom on the holistic nature of health, emphasising the interconnectedness of body, mind and spirit. According to the teachings associated with him, true healing occurs when these three components are in harmony.

One of the Archangel's main methods of promoting healing is to help people access and release old emotional traumas that may be causing energetic blockages or physical illness. He does this by illuminating inner shadows with his purifying light and guiding people through a process of understanding and reconciliation with their past.

He is also invoked in healing meditation practices. During these meditations, practitioners usually visualise Metatron's light, a bright, healing light, enveloping them and penetrating the areas of the body or mind that need healing. This light is said to act on a cellular level, promoting regeneration and revitalisation.

As well as helping with healing, Metatron is also seen as a healer of situations and places. His energy can be called upon to purify environments, dispel negative energies and restore a state of balance and peace. This is particularly important in places that have suffered trauma or are often the scene of tension and conflict.

Its influence is also sought in complementary and holistic therapies. Therapists working with Reiki, crystal therapy and other forms of energy healing often turn to Metatron to enhance their treatments, as his presence increases the effectiveness of the techniques used, helping to align the chakras and remove energy blockages.

Metatron's healing teachings also address the importance of self-acceptance and self-love. He teaches that many physical illnesses and emotional imbalances stem from a lack of inner harmony and the rejection of parts of oneself. The Archangel encourages everyone to look within with honesty and compassion, understanding that healing usually begins with self-acceptance and forgiveness of perceived faults.

Another fundamental aspect of healing is connecting with nature. He suggests that regular contact with the natural world can be profoundly healing, as the earth has an inherent capacity for restoration and renewal. Nature walks, outdoor meditation and gardening are some of the activities recommended for those seeking healing.

The archangel is also known for his ability to intercede for the sick during times of prayer and ritual. Many believers report miracles and unexplained healings after asking for his help. These stories not only reinforce the belief in his ability to heal, but also contribute to the understanding that healing can occur in mysterious and often unconventional ways.

In spiritual practice, her figure is often associated with healing through specific prayers and invocations. These prayers are used to ask not only for relief from physical illness, but also for emotional and spiritual healing. It is believed that by reciting these prayers with faith and concentration, a person can channel healing energy directly to where it is most needed.

A fundamental component of these practices is clear intention and visualisation. The associated teachings emphasise the importance of visualising the healing energy permeating any part of the body or situation that requires attention. This visualisation technique not only focuses the mind, but also activates the body's own ability to heal itself by aligning it with healing frequencies.

Metatron is also seen as a guide for those going through long healing processes. He offers patience and understanding, reminding them that healing is usually a process and that every step along the way is important. This perspective helps people in recovery to maintain a positive outlook and to understand that every moment of difficulty is also an opportunity for growth and learning.

Healing with Metatron also involves balancing the emotional and mental systems. At a time when stress and anxiety are prevalent, healing techniques inspired by the Archangel offer a form of relief and restoration. Guided meditations using his invocation help to calm the mind, reduce stress and promote a sense of inner peace.

In addition, Metatron encourages community healing, suggesting that healing efforts have better results when supported by a caring and supportive community. He promotes the idea that community environments where people can share their experiences and challenges are essential for holistic healing, as they not only provide emotional support but also strengthen the network of shared healing energy.

In addition to individual and community approaches to healing, Metatron is also revered for his ability to connect practitioners to the higher spiritual dimensions where healing takes place on a deeper and more transformative level. This aspect of his intercession is particularly valued by those who practice advanced forms of meditation and spiritual seeking.

Through these practices, followers often report experiences of spiritual ascension where they encounter visions and messages that have direct implications for their healing and personal development. These experiences are seen not only as healing, but also as opportunities to receive direct guidance on how to apply spiritual insights in everyday life to promote healing and balance.

Metatron is often described in sacred texts as a being of intense light whose presence can purify and revitalise those who invoke him. This quality is particularly important in healing contexts, where his 'light' is invoked to dissolve shadows of illness, doubt or imbalance. Practitioners use visualisations in which this light envelops the body or mind, cleansing and energising every cell and thought.

Within the spectrum of his influence, the Archangel is also recognised for his ability to intercede in cases of serious imbalance, whether spiritual, emotional or physical. His interventions are considered to be powerfully transformative, capable of radically altering the course of health conditions and guiding people back onto the path of integral health.

Metatron's role as a healer is complemented by his ability to teach people how to maintain their own health and well-being through spiritual knowledge and practice. He not only intervenes in moments of crisis, but also offers teachings that enable people to maintain their balance and harmony, thus preventing future health problems.

Metatron's ability to offer healing is widely recognised through his association with ancient knowledge and esoteric practices. He is seen as the guardian of ancient healing secrets and methods that have been passed down from generation to generation, some of which date back to biblical times, and are integrated into modern holistic practices.

The essence of healing through therapy also involves helping people to recognise themselves and align with their soul's purpose. This alignment often leads to profound healing as it allows the person to live more authentically and truthfully with their inner self, promoting a state of health and well-being that permeates all aspects of their life.

Metatron also emphasises the importance of the energy of love and forgiveness as powerful healing tools. He teaches that many physical and spiritual illnesses arise from emotional blockages and held resentments. By promoting love and forgiveness, whether through guided meditations or direct teachings, he helps to release these blockages, facilitating deeper and more lasting healing.

The Archangel is also considered a master of distance healing. He can be called upon by professionals to send healing energy to people who are not physically present. This practice is particularly valuable in times when the need for healing transcends geographical barriers, allowing spiritual help to reach those in need wherever they are in the world.

Metatron's influence in the field of spiritual and physical healing is testament to his position as a bridge between the divine and the human. His ability to bring healing is not only a reflection of his celestial power, but also of his deep commitment to the welfare of humanity. He serves not only as a healer, but also as a guide who accompanies each person on their journey back to wholeness and harmony.

Chapter Ten
Spiritual Enlightenment

Among the many attributes of this powerful archangel, perhaps one of the highest and most sacred is his ability to lead people to spiritual enlightenment. He helps individuals and communities reach deeper levels of spiritual understanding, illuminating the paths that lead to truth and divine knowledge.

Metatron is often associated with the Tree of Life, a Kabbalistic concept that symbolises the structure of the universe and the process of creation. His proximity to the divine throne and his role as celestial scribe make him an exceptional guide for those seeking to understand the deepest mysteries of existence. He is seen as a facilitator of access to the higher spheres of knowledge, helping scholars and mystics navigate the complex paths of spirituality.

The journey to spiritual enlightenment usually begins with self-knowledge. The Archangel encourages individuals to go deeper within themselves, confronting and integrating their shadows in order to gain a fuller understanding of their own being. This inner process is crucial, for the true human being is what they are. This inner process is crucial because true enlightenment comes from the harmony between self-knowledge and an understanding of the cosmos.

Metatron also teaches the importance of meditation and prayer as tools for achieving enlightenment. He guides practitioners to use these practices not only as a means of communicating with the Divine, but also as a means of transforming consciousness and perceiving higher realities. Meditations led by Metatron usually involve visualisations of light and energy rising through the chakras, purifying them and activating a direct connection with the Divine.

In addition to individual practices, Metatron is known for influencing large-scale spiritual movements and awakenings. He acts as a catalysing force at times of great spiritual transformation, when communities or even entire societies are ready to ascend to a new level of consciousness. His role in these transitions is to strengthen the spiritual energy network and ensure that the changes take place according to divine plans.

In the quest for spiritual enlightenment, Metatron often introduces practitioners to the concept of "spiritual awakening", which is a process of recognising and accepting one's own inherent divinity and intrinsic connection to the universe. He guides people through this awakening, helping them to dissolve the illusions of the ego and realise the true essence of their soul.

The Archangel teaches that enlightenment is not a state of arrival, but a continuous process of growth and expansion of consciousness. He encourages a constant approach to learning in which each experience and revelation is seen as a step on the evolutionary path of the spirit. This vision helps practitioners to keep an open mind and a heart willing to receive new lessons.

To facilitate this process, Metatron offers tools and knowledge that enable people to clear their spiritual path of obstacles and barriers. He presents energetic practices that help to clear the auric field, balance the chakras and strengthen the spiritual connection, which in turn improves the ability to receive and interpret divine messages clearly.

An important aspect of Metatron's guidance for enlightenment is the integration of the divine into everyday life. He emphasises that spirituality should not be separated from daily activities, but that every action and decision should be infused with awareness and presence. This includes practices such as mindfulness, gratitude and service to others, which are ways of manifesting spirituality in a practical and tangible way.

Metatron also addresses the importance of human relationships as part of the path to enlightenment. He teaches that interactions with other people are valuable opportunities for spiritual practice, offering opportunities to practice compassion, forgiveness and unconditional love. These values are fundamental to spiritual growth and are promoted by Metatron as essential for anyone seeking a deeper understanding of spiritual life.

Metatron encourages practitioners to explore different spiritual and philosophical traditions to enrich their journey of enlightenment. He emphasises that truth can be found in many paths and that openness to different perspectives can lead to a fuller understanding of the Divine and of oneself. This spiritual eclecticism is seen as a strength, allowing for a more inclusive and integrated view of spirituality.

Another relevant aspect is the link between spiritual enlightenment and ecological responsibility. It teaches that caring for the planet is a reflection of caring for one's own spirit, as everything is interconnected. Thus, practices that promote sustainability and respect for the environment are also spiritual practices, contributing to harmony in the world and facilitating the process of personal enlightenment.

Metatron is also known for providing experiences of the 'dark night of the soul', moments of great challenge and introspection that are crucial for spiritual growth. He guides people through these periods, helping them to confront and overcome their inner shadows.

Although these periods are difficult, Metatron presents them as valuable opportunities for purification and spiritual renewal.

The figure of the Archangel as a spiritual guide is particularly attractive to those who seek not only to understand the spiritual in a theoretical way, but also to experience it in a profound and transformative way. He offers not only knowledge, but also experiences that challenge and expand the seeker's spiritual perception.

In addition, Metatron promotes the practice of writing and study as methods of deepening spiritual enlightenment. He encourages practitioners to record their experiences and revelations, to study sacred texts and to engage in philosophical discussion as a means of consolidating and expanding their spiritual understanding.

The practice of contemplation and reflection is another fundamental pillar of Metatron's guidelines for spiritual enlightenment. He advises that moments of stillness and silence are essential to allow divine wisdom to manifest within. These moments of introspection are not just breaks in the daily routine, but real opportunities to connect with the Divine in a more intimate and profound way.

Metatron teaches that spiritual enlightenment includes the ability to see beyond appearances and to recognise the divine light in all creatures and objects.

This recognition leads to an experience of oneness with the whole universe, where the divisions and separations typical of the material world begin to dissolve.

On the path to enlightenment, Metatron emphasises the importance of resilience and perseverance. The spiritual journey is often marked by challenges and trials, and the ability to stay the course despite difficulties is crucial. The Archangel serves as a support during these times, offering his strength and protection to help seekers persevere in their quest for truth.

Metatron's influence is also key to activating spiritual gifts such as clairaudience, clairvoyance and intuition. These gifts are seen as important tools for deepening spiritual understanding and better navigating the path to enlightenment. Metatron helps people to develop these abilities, ensuring that they are used wisely and in accordance with higher spiritual goals.

The archangel also encourages a balanced approach to spiritual enlightenment, in which spiritual ascension is harmonised with earthly life. He teaches that true enlightenment does not require renunciation of the world, but a more conscious and sacred integration of spirituality into everyday life. This balance helps practitioners to live more fully and meaningfully as they continue their spiritual journey. It is essential to recognise the role of love and compassion as the foundation of this process.

Metatron teaches that divine love is the most transformative force in the universe and that cultivating a deep connection with this love is essential to achieving enlightenment. Compassion, as an expression of this love, is seen as the key to unlocking deeper levels of universal consciousness and empathy.

The Archangel also emphasises the importance of gratitude on the spiritual path. He advises that recognising and giving thanks for life's blessings creates a resonance that attracts even more divine light and wisdom. This practice of gratitude helps to keep the heart open and the mind clear, making it easier to receive new revelations and insights.

Furthermore, the journey of enlightenment with Metatron is not limited to personal, individual experiences; it also encompasses a collective dimension by encouraging the formation of spiritual communities in which members can support each other on their journeys. These communities are believed to serve as microcosms of universal harmony, reflecting the unity and interconnectedness that Metatron teaches is fundamental to the universe as a whole.

The Archangel is also a great proponent of teaching and sharing knowledge. He inspires seekers to pass on what they have learned about the spiritual path, spreading light and knowledge to others. This transmission of wisdom not only helps others to progress on their own journeys, but also solidifies the teacher's own learning and understanding.

Spiritual enlightenment under Metatron's tutelage is an invitation to a transformative journey that goes beyond self-improvement to a broader contribution to the world. Metatron guides each person to become a beacon of light whose own enlightenment can inspire and uplift others around them, fostering a wider and deeper spiritual awakening.

Chapter Eleven
Spiritual Teachings

One of the main focuses of Metatron's teachings is the connection between the microcosm and the macrocosm, how individual reality reflects universal reality. He teaches that every soul is a reflection of the Divine and that by understanding one's own nature, the individual can understand the Universe. This lesson is fundamental to developing a broader perception of yourself and the world around you.

The Archangel is also known for his ability to impart knowledge of the spiritual laws that govern the cosmos. He explains how these laws affect everyday life and how actions and thoughts can be aligned with them to live more harmoniously and effectively. His teachings help practitioners navigate life with greater wisdom and purpose.

In addition to universal laws, he discusses topics such as the nature of time and space, the interconnectedness of all things, and the importance of consciousness in creating reality. He reveals how consciousness shapes the fabric of reality and how, by altering one's perception, it is possible to influence the environment and events.

Metatron also addresses the duality of existence and teaches how to integrate seemingly opposing aspects of life, such as light and shadow, joy and pain. He encourages his followers to recognise and accept all aspects of themselves and the world, showing that true spiritual understanding comes from synthesis and integration, not from the rejection of certain elements of existence.

Another teaching speaks of the importance of pure intention and conscious action in spiritual practice. It emphasises that the intentions behind actions are as important as the actions themselves, and profoundly influence the energetic and spiritual results. This principle is vital for anyone seeking to live a life aligned with higher spiritual values.

He also explores the dynamics of karma and reincarnation, explaining how the actions and choices of one life can influence the circumstances and lessons of future lives. He offers guidance on how to resolve past karmas and how to live in a way that promotes spiritual growth and minimises future karmic complications.

An important aspect of his teachings is the promotion of peace and understanding between different cultures and spiritual traditions. He argues that at the heart of all religious and spiritual practices are universal truths that can unite humanity. Metatron encourages interfaith dialogue and respect as the basis for building a more harmonious and spiritually integrated world.

He is also a master at explaining the complexity of the higher spiritual planes and how human beings can connect with these higher realities, offering meditation and contemplation techniques that help practitioners transcend the limitations of the physical world and experience more subtle and spiritually rich dimensions of existence.

In addition to spiritual practices and concepts, Metatron emphasises the development of compassion and selfless service. He teaches that service to others is one of the highest expressions of spirituality and a powerful form of personal evolution. Through service, individuals can not only help alleviate suffering in the world, but also cultivate divine qualities within themselves, such as love, patience and generosity.

The Archangel also teaches about the connection between the mind, body and spirit, emphasising the importance of keeping each aspect healthy and integrated. He reveals how imbalances in one can affect all the others, and offers holistic healing practices designed to restore harmony between these three pillars of the human being.

In his teachings he often discusses the power of the spoken word and sound, teaching that words have a creative power and that sound, especially in forms such as mantras and chants, can be used to balance and align the energies of the body and mind. This knowledge is applied in both healing practices and meditation, where sound is used as a vehicle to reach deeper states of consciousness.

Metatron emphasises the need to develop spiritual discipline through regular and consistent practice. He advises that transformation and enlightenment are the result of an ongoing commitment to spiritual growth, not sporadic experiences. Regularity in meditation, study and other spiritual practices strengthens the connection with the Divine and stabilises the transformations achieved.

The archangel also addresses the concept of spiritual freedom, explaining that true freedom is the ability to act in harmony with the divine will without being guided by selfish desires or fears. Metatron teaches how to identify and overcome the inner barriers that prevent this freedom, encouraging a life of authenticity and purpose.

Metatron discusses the importance of humility on the spiritual path. He warns that pride and ego can be major obstacles on the journey of spiritual growth, and that maintaining an attitude of humility allows for the continued reception of divine graces and teachings.

He emphasises the importance of perseverance on the spiritual path and stresses that challenges and trials are not only inevitable but essential to spiritual development. These challenges are seen as opportunities to strengthen faith, deepen understanding and practice spiritual resilience. The Archangel advises his followers to face these difficulties with courage and confidence, reminding them that each obstacle overcome is a step forward on the evolutionary journey.

The practice of introspection is another essential tool taught. It encourages people to engage in regular self-examination and deep reflection to better understand their motivations, desires and fears. This practice not only aids self-understanding and personal growth, but also sets the stage for positive and transformative changes in behaviour and attitude.

The Archangel is also an advocate of justice and fairness, teaching that true spirituality is reflected in the way we treat others and strive to create a more just and equitable world. He instructs his followers to act as agents of change, promoting peace, equality and respect for all forms of life.

Metatron also discusses the connection between spirituality and art. He sees artistic expression as a powerful form of meditation and connection with the divine. Through music, painting, writing and other art forms, individuals can explore and express their spiritual experiences, creating a bridge between the material and spiritual worlds.

He also teaches the importance of maintaining a sense of purpose and direction. He advises his followers to set clear spiritual goals and consciously work towards them, in accordance with the values and teachings that promote the growth and expansion of the soul.

In his role as a spiritual mentor, Metatron also teaches the importance of adaptation and flexibility in spiritual practice. He emphasises that while consistency is crucial, the ability to adapt to new information and circumstances is equally important for spiritual growth. He encourages practitioners to be open to new ideas and to integrate new knowledge into their spiritual paths, always maintaining a balance between tradition and innovation.

He also emphasises the need for spiritual protection. He offers teachings on how to strengthen the auric field and protect oneself from negative influences or harmful energies. This aspect of spiritual practice is fundamental to maintaining integrity and clarity in the spiritual journey.

Metatron also addresses the subject of death and the afterlife. He provides a comforting insight into the continuity of the soul and the journey after physical death, and offers guidance on how to live a life that prepares the soul for the transitions after death. These teachings help to reduce the fear of death and to see the transition as a natural part of the cycle of existence.

In his teachings he often uses parables and stories to illustrate complex spiritual principles in an accessible way. These stories help followers visualise abstract concepts and apply them to their lives in a practical and meaningful way.

He also encourages the practice of prayer and celebration as ways of maintaining an ongoing connection with the Divine, teaching that prayers, rituals and festivals not only honour the Divine, but also strengthen the network of spiritual connections that support the individual's journey and strengthen the community of faith.

Chapter Twelve
Dimensions

Metatron, the Archangel, is an entity that transcends common understanding, operating in various dimensions ranging from the physical to the spiritual and metaphysical. His existence allows him to act as a bridge between the divine and the mundane, influencing both the heavenly and earthly realms. He is often described in mystical traditions as a being who inhabits the threshold between the visible and the invisible, able to navigate the different planes of existence with an ease that no other celestial being possesses. This unique quality makes Metatron a central figure in many esoteric beliefs, where he is seen both as the guardian of divine knowledge and as a mediator between God and humanity.

In the earthly realm, Metatron influences world events and individual lives, often in ways that remain hidden from our limited perception. He directs the flow of spiritual energy to shape events on a macroscopic level, influencing the direction of humanity's spiritual evolution.

At the same time, in the celestial realm, Metatron directs all cosmic events according to divine plan. He is one of the few beings who can withstand the immediate presence of God without being consumed, a testament to his closeness and importance to the divine throne.

In addition to his work in the heavenly and earthly realms, Metatron serves as a spiritual guide for those seeking wisdom. He offers enlightenment and guidance to those who seek to understand the deepest mysteries of existence. Through his intercession, many mystics and sages have received revelations and insights that have profoundly altered their perceptions and, by extension, their lives.

Metatron's multidimensional nature makes him a unique figure in the spiritual pantheon. His ability to operate on different levels of reality highlights him not only as a being of immense power, but also as a being of immense wisdom and compassion. By understanding the different dimensions of his existence, we begin to appreciate the complexity and depth of his role in the cosmos.

The Archangel's ability to influence both the celestial and the terrestrial underscores his function as the keeper of the cosmic balance. Not only does he mediate the spiritual interactions that affect the universe, but he also ensures that the balance between mercy and justice is maintained in all spheres. This colossal responsibility underscores his importance as one of the pillars of the cosmic order.

As a being who exists in several dimensions, he has the unique task of interceding on behalf of different realities. His presence is invoked in spiritual rituals that seek not only protection, but also the cleansing and energetic alignment of spaces. He is able to channel energies from higher dimensions to assist in healing and spiritual transformation, acting as a catalyst for spiritual growth and general wellbeing.

Metatron plays a crucial role in revealing esoteric secrets to the chosen ones. He is believed to hold the keys to many of the most closely guarded secrets of the universe. Through his guidance, individuals are able to access deeper layers of knowledge and understanding, often receiving revelations that transcend conventional knowledge and take them to new heights of spiritual enlightenment.

His unique position as one of the highest archangels gives him unparalleled divine authority. He is often referred to as "Little YHWH", an allusion to his closeness and resemblance to the Divine. This nomenclature reflects not only his immense power and wisdom, but also his role as the executor of the divine will, enforcing heavenly laws and ensuring that order is maintained at all levels of creation.

Understanding Metatron's multiple dimensions allows us to realise the breadth and depth of his impact on the cosmos. He is not only a spiritual authority figure; he is also a guide and protector whose influence extends to all aspects of existence. Recognising his contributions to universal balance and harmony helps us to better understand the complexity of spiritual and material life.

Metatron not only fulfils divine laws; he is also charged with overseeing the application of these laws throughout the universe. This role makes him one of the most respected and feared of the celestial beings. He ensures that balance and order are maintained not only in the interactions between celestial beings, but also in the energetic manifestations that affect the physical world.

Metatron's ability to mediate conflict extends across all dimensions. Whether resolving disputes between angels or intervening in complex human issues, his ability to bring clarity and peace is unparalleled. He uses his profound wisdom to navigate delicate situations, ensuring that any resolution is in line with justice and truth.

The Archangel also plays a crucial role in maintaining cosmic harmony. He coordinates the forces that keep the stars and planets in motion, ensuring that the universe operates according to a meticulously orchestrated divine plan. His vision and intervention are essential in preventing cosmic chaos and facilitating the cycles of creation and destruction that are natural to the universe.

In addition to his administrative and judicial functions, he is a spiritual teacher who guides souls on their journey of Ascension. He offers teachings that illuminate the path to greater spiritual understanding, encouraging introspection and personal growth. Those who follow his advice are usually able to transcend their earthly limitations and reach higher states of consciousness.

Metatron's ability to influence universal laws and cosmic order illustrates the extent of his power and his importance in the fabric of the cosmos. As guardian of the laws and teacher of wisdom, he serves as a central pillar for maintaining harmony between all forms of life and existence. Through his guidance, beings from many worlds find their way to enlightenment and a deep understanding of the structure of reality.

The Archangel occupies a unique place in the cosmos as the link between the divine and the human. He facilitates communication and interaction between these two worlds, acting as a messenger and mediator. His duties include delivering divine messages to prophets and spiritual leaders, as well as guiding human souls on their spiritual path.

Metatron not only transmits divine wisdom, but also guides humans in the practical application of these teachings. He is often seen as a mentor to mystics and spiritualists, teaching techniques that allow individuals to access higher energies and gain a deeper understanding of their own spiritual nature.

In esoteric and mystical practices, he is invoked in rituals designed to purify, protect and uplift. He is called upon to sanctify sacred spaces, bless ceremonies and strengthen barriers against negative energies. Metatron's presence is considered extremely powerful, capable of significantly altering the energetic vibrations of an environment or a person.

In addition to his more visible functions, Metatron is also the guardian of occult knowledge. He holds the keys to ancient mysteries and is responsible for selecting those who are ready to receive profound esoteric secrets. Through his guidance, knowledge that has been hidden for eons is revealed to worthy initiates, promoting significant spiritual advancement.

Metatron's presence at the intersection of the spiritual and material worlds demonstrates his transcendental importance. Not only does he serve as a bridge for the flow of divine wisdom, but he also ensures that this wisdom is accessible and understandable to human beings seeking spiritual growth. He is therefore not just an archangel, but an essential facilitator of humanity's spiritual journey.

Metatron is unique among celestial beings in his ability to manifest not only spiritually, but also perceptibly in the physical world. He influences events and circumstances in ways that often go unnoticed, but his interventions are crucial to the balance and spiritual evolution of the planet.

It is said that he can be felt and even observed in natural phenomena that carry a spiritual charge, such as the Northern Lights, eclipses and places of energetic power on Earth. These manifestations are seen as signs of his presence and blessing, and serve as a reminder of the connection between heaven and earth.

Although his work is generally subtle, he has been known to influence large-scale world events. He can direct cosmic energies to promote peace, healing and justice, or to awaken humanity to the changes needed in times of global crisis.

One of his most important functions in the physical world is to facilitate collective spiritual awakening. He guides the energies of consciousness evolution, helping societies to reach new heights of understanding and compassion. This is done not only through spiritual leaders and masters, but also through cultural movements that promote awareness and spiritual transformation.

Chapter Thirteen
The Archangel and Humanity

Metatron is a figure that transcends cultural barriers and is revered in various spiritual traditions around the world. From ancient civilisations to modern times, he is seen as a divine messenger, spiritual guide and protector of humanity.

In Judaism and Christianity, he is often associated with the prophet Enoch, who was elevated to the status of archangel after his ascension to heaven. This association emphasises his closeness to God and his role as a heavenly scribe recording the deeds of humanity. He is revered as a powerful intercessor, able to bring the prayers of the faithful directly to the divine throne.

In Islam, although he is not explicitly mentioned by name, there are analogous figures who perform similar functions as intermediaries between God and the prophets. Metatron's influence as a spiritual guide is similar to that of the angels, who deliver divine messages and offer protection and guidance to human beings on their spiritual journey.

Although less well known in Eastern traditions, the concept of a celestial being who mediates communication between heaven and earth is found in various Asian philosophies and spiritual practices. In some interpretations, Metatron is seen as a bodhisattva, a being who seeks enlightenment not only for himself but for all sentient beings.

In indigenous communities around the world, similar figures are revered as great spirits or ancestors who serve as guardians and guides. In these cultures he is often associated with nature and the protection of the environment, emphasising his role in maintaining the balance between the physical and spiritual worlds.

Metatron's ability to manifest in so many different traditions underlines his importance as a truly universal archangel. His role as guide and protector is a recurring theme that resonates with the human desire for connection and understanding of the divine. Throughout the ages he has been a beacon of hope and wisdom for humanity, guiding the faithful on their spiritual journeys.

Metatron is often seen as a spiritual mentor, guiding individuals and communities on their journey of spiritual development. His ability to provide wise counsel and support is vital to those seeking greater understanding and connection with the Divine.

One of his most important functions, as we are constantly reminded, is to serve as an intercessor between humans and the Divine. He facilitates the communication of human prayers and desires with the heavenly realm, ensuring that petitions are heard and answered according to the divine will. This intercession is especially valued in times of great need and despair, when his presence and help can be perceived as miraculous.

At times of great personal or collective transition, Metatron is invoked to offer his protection and wisdom. Whether at birth, death or during significant life changes, his presence is seen as a support for safe passage through these portals of transformation.

In addition to his mediating functions, Metatron is also an educator of virtues and spiritual values. He teaches the importance of integrity, compassion and justice, and guides souls to live according to these high principles. These teachings were created to uplift not only the individual but also society as a whole, promoting a culture of peace and mutual respect.

Metatron inspires people not only with words, but also with profound spiritual experiences. Many who report encounters with Metatron describe feeling an intense light and warmth, sensations that bring peace, clarity and a renewed purpose to life. These experiences often lead to a new or renewed commitment to spiritual paths and a desire to help others.

The Archangel's work as a spiritual guide and mentor highlights his ability to positively influence the spiritual path of humanity. Through his knowledge and compassion, he helps to shape not only individuals but also the course of entire cultures, leading them to a deeper and more harmonious understanding of the cosmos and their own existence.

Metatron is a figure who appears under different names and aspects in various religious and spiritual traditions around the world. This ability reveals his importance as a facilitator of communication and understanding between heaven and earth, and between different cultures and beliefs.

As mentioned above, although not a central figure in Buddhism, the concept of Metatron can be compared to that of the Bodhisattvas, beings who have attained enlightenment but have chosen to remain in the cycle of samsara in order to help all beings achieve liberation. This comparison illustrates how Metatron acts in a similar capacity, guiding souls to higher levels of consciousness and understanding.

In Hindu mythology, figures such as Narada, a divine sage and messenger between the gods and humans, share many characteristics with Metatron. They act as a bridge between the divine and the mundane, bringing important messages and guiding devotees on their spiritual path.

In the spiritual traditions of Africa and the Americas, similar beings are invoked for protection, guidance and as mediators between the spiritual and physical worlds. These figures are fundamental to ritual practices and are respected as guardians of ancestral knowledge and wisdom.

Metatron, with his ability to appear in different forms and traditions, is a perfect example of how spiritual concepts can transcend religious and cultural boundaries. He is a figure who can unite people of different faiths, promoting interfaith dialogue and mutual understanding.

His presence in different spiritual traditions around the world not only reinforces his role as a figure of universal significance, but also demonstrates how spiritual truths can be found and respected in different cultures and beliefs. He is a symbol of unity in diversity, showing that the search for enlightenment and divine understanding is a common theme for all humanity.

Metatron plays a crucial role in times of significant change on Earth. He is seen as a catalyst for spiritual and social change, helping humanity to face global challenges with wisdom and compassion. His influence is felt in movements that seek peace, social justice and harmony between peoples.

In times of crisis, whether natural disaster, conflict or pandemic, he is often called upon to offer comfort and guidance. He helps alleviate fear and uncertainty and inspires leaders and individuals to act with integrity and courage. His presence is a reminder that greater forces are at work, guiding human efforts towards a positive resolution.

Metatron is also considered a protector of the environment, influencing awareness of sustainability and conservation. He encourages a more respectful and caring relationship with the planet, emphasising the interdependence of all life forms and the importance of maintaining ecological balance.

Metatron is a figure who transcends cultural and religious barriers, promoting international understanding and cooperation. He inspires leaders and communities to seek solutions that respect diversity and promote global peace. His influence is particularly valued in peace negotiations and in forums where cooperation between nations and cultures is crucial.

The Archangel's ability to influence global events and inspire positive change is a testament to his power and dedication to humanity. He not only guides people on their personal journeys, but also has a tangible impact on large-scale issues that affect entire communities and nations. Metatron continues to be a force for good, guiding the world through its most challenging times with a firm hand and a compassionate heart.

As well as being a figure of cosmic grandeur, he is also deeply relevant to the daily lives of spiritual seekers. Through prayer and meditation practices, many devotees feel Metatron's presence, gently guiding them and offering insights that illuminate their spiritual path. The constant practice of these connections strengthens the relationship between human beings and the Divine, facilitated by Metatron's intercession.

The figure of Metatron transcends the spiritual to influence art and culture. Artists of all kinds, from writers to musicians and painters, find in him a spiritual muse. Inspired works often have a depth that touches on the divine, opening new perspectives for art lovers and elevating the collective spirit.

Metatron is seen as a spiritual educator whose teachings transcend formal religious traditions and reach all who are open to spiritual growth. Esoteric schools and spiritual study groups use the teachings attributed to Metatron to create curricula that promote the development of consciousness and a deeper understanding of existence.

Metatron's influence also extends to social movements fighting for justice, equality and change. His energy is invoked in campaigns for human rights and environmental sustainability, strengthening the moral and spiritual drive of activists and giving them resilience and clarity of purpose.

Metatron's legacy is a rich tapestry of celestial and earthly interactions. Throughout the ages his figure has been a source of light, wisdom and protection. As we continue to explore and understand his multi-dimensionality, it becomes clear that Metatron is more than an archangel; he is an eternal symbol of the human potential to transcend the tangible and touch the divine. His ongoing relationship with humanity is a reminder that spirituality is a shared journey, enriched by the guidance and presence of this powerful celestial leader.

Chapter Fourteen
Metatron's Teachings

Metatron is revered not only as a messenger between the divine and the human, but also as a teacher whose teachings have profoundly influenced spirituality in various cultures. This chapter explores Metatron's specific teachings, focusing on how they guide followers in their quest for enlightenment and spiritual understanding.

The Archangel teaches that spiritual understanding comes not only through study, but also through direct experience with the Divine. He emphasises the importance of prayer, meditation and spiritual practice as a means of achieving a deeper connection with the sacred. These principles were created to help people transcend the material and discover the universal truths that unite all existences.

One of the recurring themes in his teachings is the search for balance and harmony between the physical and the spiritual. He advises his followers to cultivate a life that respects the needs of both body and mind and promotes a state of well-being that is essential for spiritual growth.

He often discusses the law of karma, teaching that every action has a corresponding reaction in the universe, and instructs his followers to live with awareness and responsibility, always aware of the consequences of their actions in both the material and spiritual worlds.

His teachings place great emphasis on compassion and forgiveness. He teaches that true spiritual progress cannot occur without an open heart, willing to forgive others and oneself. Compassion is seen as a transformative force that can alleviate suffering and bring inner peace.

Metatron's teachings offer a rich and profound path for those seeking greater understanding and connection with the Divine. Through his words, he guides believers on a journey of self-discovery and transformation, emphasising the importance of living a life that reflects the highest spiritual values.

Metatron is considered a master of esoteric mysteries, offering his followers knowledge beyond common understanding. He reveals the hidden structures of the universe and how they affect spiritual and material life. Metatron's teachings cover topics such as the nature of the soul, the interconnectedness of all things and the secrets of divine creation.

Metatron instructs his students in advanced spiritual practices that facilitate access to higher states of consciousness. These practices include deep meditation, visualisation and the use of mantras that resonate with divine frequencies. These practices not only raise consciousness, but also help to purify the being, preparing it to receive deeper truths.

One of the main themes of Metatron's teachings is the concept of duality and unity. He explains how the apparent dualities of the world, such as light and shadow, good and evil, are actually aspects of a single interconnected reality. Understanding this unity is essential to achieving inner peace and harmony with the environment.

Metatron also guides his followers through spiritual challenges, teaching them to face and overcome the trials that are part of spiritual growth. He emphasises the importance of maintaining faith and determination, even in the most difficult situations, as a way of strengthening the spirit and progressing on the spiritual journey.

Metatron's teachings also address ethical and moral issues, emphasising the importance of living a life that reflects spiritual principles. He instils in his followers the need to act with integrity, justice and altruism, seeing these qualities not only as moral virtues but as fundamental to spiritual evolution.

Metatron's teachings are an invitation to explore the depths of the spirit and to engage in an ongoing search for wisdom and enlightenment. Through his guidance, he provides tools for navigating the complex spiritual world and encourages his followers to live according to the highest spiritual truths.

Metatron is a herald of the expansion of consciousness, offering teachings that not only educate but also transform. He emphasises the importance of broadening our perception beyond physical and mental limitations to gain a broader understanding of our true spiritual potential.

One of the main focuses of Metatron's teachings is the integration of spirituality into everyday life. He teaches his followers how to maintain a constant connection with the Divine, even in the midst of mundane activities. This is achieved through the constant practice of mindfulness, prayer and meditation, transforming every action into an expression of faith and spiritual purpose.

Metatron often teaches about the chakras, with particular emphasis on the third eye and crown chakra, which are centres of perception and spiritual connection. He offers specific practices to activate and harmonise these chakras, facilitating experiences of enlightenment and deeper connections with higher spiritual realities.

Metatron helps to understand cosmic cycles and their impact on the spiritual journey. He explains how astrological movements and cosmic epochs influence spiritual evolution and how we can align our lives with these universal rhythms to optimise our growth and understanding.

One of Metatron's most profound teachings is about the illusory nature of physical reality and the true essence of being. He challenges conventional concepts of existence and guides us as to what reality is. He challenges conventional concepts of existence and leads his followers to the understanding that everything we perceive is a manifestation of divine consciousness.

Through Metatron's teachings we are invited to explore previously unimaginable spiritual depths. He guides us to live more consciously and in alignment with the Universe, showing us that every moment is an opportunity to perceive and manifest our true divine nature. These teachings are not only enlightening but also empowering, offering new perspectives on how to live in harmony with the cosmos.

One of the pillars of Metatron's teachings is the understanding of the interconnectedness of all things in the universe. He teaches that every being, every event and every thought is intrinsically linked to the cosmic fabric, influencing and being influenced by a common energy field.

Metatron emphasises the idea of unity, showing that beyond the apparent physical and spiritual separations, everything is part of an indivisible whole. This vision promotes a deep sense of empathy and responsibility, where the wellbeing of one is seen as essential to the wellbeing of all.

To facilitate the understanding of universal oneness, Metatron teaches a variety of spiritual practices. These practices include guided meditations that focus on dissolving ego barriers and promoting a direct experience of connection with all that exists.

Metatron also discusses how each individual action has a significant impact on the collective. He urges his followers to act with awareness, considering the ramifications of their choices and behaviours not only for themselves, but for the world around them.

By emphasising selfless service, Metatron encourages attitudes and actions that promote cooperation and mutual support. He teaches that service to others is one of the highest expressions of spirituality and a direct path to spiritual development.

Metatron's teachings on universal interconnectedness are fundamental to promoting a more just, compassionate and spiritually awakened society. By living according to these principles, individuals can contribute to a world of harmony and mutual understanding, reflecting the true unity that Metatron reveals.

Metatron transmits teachings that not only address the expansion of consciousness, but also emphasise the importance of spiritual ethics. He instructs his followers to live in a way that reflects the highest values of integrity, honesty and altruism, emphasising that these qualities are essential for true spiritual evolution.

Metatron's teachings emphasise that ethics cannot be separated from spiritual practice. True spirituality involves a commitment to an ethical life in which decisions and actions are always considered in the light of their spiritual and material consequences.

Metatron teaches that each individual has a universal responsibility, not only for their actions, but also for their omissions. He encourages an active life in the pursuit of justice and fairness, promoting the idea that each person has a role to play in the healing and progress of the world.

Another central aspect of Metatron's teachings is the practice of forgiveness and reconciliation. He argues that forgiveness is one of the most powerful forces for personal and collective transformation, capable of resolving conflict and healing old wounds on both a personal and global level.

Metatron emphasises that spiritual teachings must be experienced in everyday life, not just understood in theory. He suggests practical actions that anyone can take to manifest these spiritual values in their lives, such as random acts of kindness, volunteering and other forms of community service.

Metatron's teachings challenge us to seek a life that is not only spiritually enlightened but also ethically powerful. By integrating these principles into our lives, we can contribute to a more just and compassionate world that is truly aligned with the visions of unity and interconnectedness that Metatron reveals.

Chapter Fifteen
Esoteric Sciences

Metatron is a central figure in many esoteric traditions, where he is seen as a master of occult realities and a guide to the mystical understanding of the universe. This chapter explores how Metatron is integrated into the esoteric sciences, such as astrology, numerology and alchemy, and what his role is in these practices.

In astrology, Metatron is often associated with the regulation of cosmic energies that affect human destiny. He helps practitioners to understand planetary movements and their subtle effects on the human psyche and behaviour, offering essential insights for spiritual and material alignment.

In numerology, Metatron is considered the guardian of the numerical secrets that structure the universe. It is believed that he provides the key to understanding the vibrations and energies that each number emanates, helping practitioners to decipher the hidden patterns of existence and use this information to bring harmony and understanding to their lives.

In alchemy, Metatron is seen as a symbol of transformation and purification. He guides alchemists in their quest to transform raw materials into substances of great spiritual and material value, symbolising the transmutation of the lead of ignorance into the gold of spiritual knowledge.

Metatron also plays an important role in various forms of magical practice, where he is invoked for protection, purification and enlightenment. His symbols and sigils are used as tools to channel high energies and perform rituals that seek to influence the natural course of events or expand spiritual awareness.

Metatron's presence in the esoteric sciences demonstrates his importance as a mediator of occult knowledge and a guide for those who seek to understand the mystical depths of the universe. His teachings and influence are essential to the practice of these disciplines, providing a bridge between ancient knowledge and contemporary applications.

Metatron is seen as a portal to occult knowledge, providing access to information beyond common understanding. He acts as a master who instructs esoteric practitioners on how to access and interpret the hidden truths that shape the universe.

In the Kabbalah tradition, Metatron is seen as the highest of the angels, responsible for the transmission of divine and mystical knowledge. He is associated with the Sephirot of the Crown, representing the direct connection to the source of all creation and the manifestation of divine thought in the physical world.

Metatron is often invoked in esoteric meditation practices to guide practitioners on spiritual journeys that reveal the hidden aspects of reality. These meditations can include astral journeys, visions of alternate realities and encounters with higher consciousness.

The ability to manipulate and understand subtle energies is another aspect of Metatron's teachings. He teaches esotericists how to channel and use these energies for healing, personal transformation and to achieve energetic balance in different environments and situations.

Metatron is known for preserving and revealing ancient secrets encoded in sacred texts, mystical symbols and geometric structures. His teachings help practitioners to decipher these codes, allowing for a deeper understanding of the laws that govern the cosmos and ancient spiritual practices.

Metatron serves as an essential guide for those involved in the esoteric sciences, not only as a transmitter of knowledge, but as a mentor who helps to navigate and apply this profound knowledge. His guidance is fundamental to unravelling the mysteries that link all aspects of spiritual and material life.

Metatron is often associated with divination practices, where he is invoked to clarify and guide the processes of obtaining visions and messages about the future or hidden truths. He assists in the accurate interpretation of symbols and signs, ensuring that the wisdom revealed is used responsibly and with integrity.

In the Tarot, Metatron is a figure that can be associated with cards of deep spiritual significance, such as The Hermit or The Star, which symbolise the search for inner knowledge and divine guidance. Tarot practitioners invoke Metatron to deepen their understanding of the readings and to connect the interpretations to the spiritual needs of the reader.

In the context of the I Ching, the Book of Changes, Metatron can be seen as a facilitator in understanding the hexagrams and interpreting their meaning in terms of energy flow and personal transformation. He helps practitioners to understand the subtle messages contained in the changes of the trigrams and to apply these teachings in daily life.

Metatron is also a guide for those who practice clairvoyance, providing clarity and protection during sessions in which visions of the past, present or future are revealed. He ensures that the messages received are interpreted with the utmost precision and that the insights are used ethically and constructively.

In esoteric astrology, which seeks to understand the spiritual influences behind astral events, Metatron is consulted to provide insight into how celestial movements reflect individual and collective spiritual paths. He guides astrologers in using this knowledge to promote spiritual growth and evolution.

Through the various forms of divination, Metatron provides a bridge between esoteric knowledge and its practical application in the physical world. His guidance ensures that practitioners not only receive messages and predictions, but also deeply understand their implications and how to use them for spiritual and material development.

Metatron is often seen as a central symbol of spiritual alchemy, a practice that seeks to transform the human spirit, raising it from a state of ignorance to a state of enlightenment. He guides alchemists in the process of purifying and transmuting their souls, teaching them how to transform low energies into higher, more divine vibrations.

Under Metatron's tutelage, practitioners of spiritual alchemy learn to manipulate and transform their inner energies. This involves deep meditation techniques, visualisation and the use of sacred symbols that facilitate spiritual transmutation. Metatron reveals how these practices can lead to the purification of the body, mind and spirit.

Metatron is associated with many alchemical symbols, such as the Caduceus, which represents duality transformed into unity and spiritual ascension. He helps practitioners understand the hidden meanings behind these symbols and guides them on their personal journeys of self-knowledge and transformation.

In the alchemical tradition, the creation of elixirs to promote health and spiritual awakening is a common practice. Metatron teaches how to combine physical and spiritual ingredients to create these potions, the aim of which is to raise consciousness and harmonise the being with cosmic energies.

Metatron teaches that alchemy is not just a series of isolated experiments, but an integrated approach to spiritual development. He encourages alchemists to see each stage of the alchemical process as a metaphor for personal and spiritual transformation, reflecting the inner work necessary to achieve true wisdom and enlightenment.

As a master of spiritual alchemy, Metatron offers a powerful path for those seeking to transform their lives through spirituality. He guides practitioners in understanding and applying alchemical principles that not only transmute the physical elements, but also catalyse profound spiritual changes that lead to fulfilment and divine awakening.

Metatron is a revered presence in various mystical traditions around the world. He is seen as the guardian of sacred knowledge and a guide for those seeking spiritual depth. This role transcends cultural and religious barriers, making him a central figure in many esoteric and mystical paths.

In Sufism, the mystical dimension of Islam, figures such as Metatron are seen as examples of beings who have achieved closeness to the divine. Although he is not explicitly mentioned, his archetype influences meditation and recitation practices aimed at union with God, demonstrating the universality of his figure.

In shamanism practised in various cultures, figures similar to Metatron are invoked to mediate communication between the spiritual and physical worlds. He is seen as an "allied spirit" who helps shamans on their spiritual journeys, offering protection and guidance.

In Hinduism and esoteric Buddhism, Metatron can be compared to deities and beings such as the Bodhisattvas, who take a vow to help all beings achieve enlightenment. His dedication to spiritual service and the upliftment of humanity is in keeping with these traditions' teachings of compassion and self-sacrifice.

In Western mystery schools such as Freemasonry and the Rosicrucians, Metatron is often involved in symbolism and rituals designed to enlighten members about the mysteries of existence. He is regarded as a master who holds the keys to the deepest spiritual and cosmological mysteries.

Metatron's presence in various mystical and esoteric traditions around the world underlines his role as a universal spiritual teacher. His ability to serve as a bridge between different spiritual paths and their diverse cultural manifestations makes his teachings a valuable resource for any mystical or esoteric practice. Metatron continues to inspire those who seek spiritual truth, guiding them through the veils of mystery to a deeper understanding of the Divine.

Chapter Sixteen
Contemporary Challenges

In a world facing rapid change and significant challenges, from environmental crises to social and political tensions, the figure of Metatron emerges as a crucial spiritual guide. This chapter explores how Metatron can be invoked and understood in contemporary contexts, and how his wisdom can be applied to address current issues.

Metatron is seen as a protector of the natural balance and is often invoked in practices aimed at environmental restoration. He offers guidance on how to live sustainably and respect the Earth's natural cycles, teaching that the health of the planet is directly linked to the spiritual health of humanity.

In times of global conflict and political uncertainty, Metatron can be a source of peace and reconciliation. He inspires leaders and individuals to seek peaceful solutions and to promote dialogue and understanding between different nations and cultures, emphasising the importance of cooperation and compassion in all human interactions.

In the context of the digital and information age, Metatron helps to navigate the vast amount of data and information, guiding people to distinguish between what is truly useful and what is distracting or misleading. He promotes a balanced approach to the use of technology, highlighting how it can be used to promote wellbeing and spiritual growth.

Metatron is also seen as a champion of social justice, offering support and guidance to movements fighting for equality and human rights. He encourages action to eliminate oppression and promote human dignity, and guides those who work to create a more just and equitable society.

With his broad perspective and deep wisdom, Metatron is an invaluable resource for addressing today's challenges. He offers not only spiritual guidance, but also practical solutions that can help solve the most pressing problems of our time and lead humanity towards a more hopeful and sustainable future.

In times of global crisis, Metatron is called upon not only as a symbol of hope, but also as an active spiritual advisor. He offers perspectives that help to understand world events as part of a larger plan, encouraging humanity to find resilience and purpose even in hardship.

During events such as pandemics, Metatron can be seen as a guide to spiritual and physical understanding of the crisis. He offers teachings on how to maintain spiritual integrity and mental health, and how communities can come together in mutual support, overcoming adversity with solidarity and compassion.

Metatron encourages deep reflection on social structures, challenging individuals to question and reform systems that do not serve the common good. He guides those who seek social change to do so with an open and just heart, always aligning their actions with the principles of truth and justice.

In situations of natural disaster, Metatron is called upon to provide comfort and renew faith. He helps affected communities find the strength to rebuild and recover, inspiring collective action based on hope and cooperation.

Metatron is a powerful ally in building community resilience, teaching how to turn adversity into opportunities for growth and unity. He emphasises the importance of cooperation and mutual support as essential elements in overcoming challenges together.

Metatron's guidance in times of crisis is a reminder that even in the most difficult of times there is the possibility of transformation and renewal. His wisdom helps us to see beyond the immediate and how each challenge can be a stepping stone to greater spiritual maturity and community cohesion.

Metatron is seen as a defender of ecological balance and sustainability. He guides people to recognise the importance of protecting the environment as an extension of their own spiritual and physical health. Through his teachings, Metatron promotes greater awareness of human impact on the planet and the need for sustainable action.

Metatron encourages the integration of spiritual practices into environmental education, suggesting that respect for the Earth is a reflection of respect for the Divine. It supports programmes and initiatives that teach how to live more harmoniously with nature, using resources responsibly and promoting conservation.

In addition to traditional practices, Metatron is associated with the promotion of green technologies that help reduce the environmental impact of human activities. He is seen as a guide for those developing and implementing new technologies that support sustainability and the health of the planet.

Metatron teaches the importance of biodiversity, emphasising how each species plays a vital role in the global ecosystem. He urges people to recognise the interdependence of all life forms and to work to protect natural habitats to ensure the continuity of life in all its forms.

Metatron's influence extends to encouraging collective action to address environmental challenges.

He inspires communities to unite in defence of the environment, promoting initiatives that combine individual and collective efforts to make a significant positive impact.

Metatron plays a vital role in environmental awareness and action, guiding humanity towards a more respectful and sustainable relationship with the Earth. His teachings are helping to shape an environmental ethic that recognises the sacredness of the natural world and human responsibility for its preservation.

In this day and age, when mental health challenges are exacerbated by factors such as social isolation and global anxiety, Metatron offers spiritual support that can be crucial to mental well-being. He guides people to find inner peace and emotional stability through spiritual practices that reduce stress and promote harmony.

Metatron is an advocate of meditation as a tool for maintaining and improving mental health. He teaches specific techniques to help calm the mind, centre the spirit and connect with calming energies. These practices are designed to strengthen mental resilience and promote a sense of lasting peace.

In addition to meditation, Metatron emphasises the importance of emotional balance. He offers guidance on how to deal with intense and conflicting emotions and provides strategies for processing them in a healthy way. These techniques include conscious reflection, artistic expression and open dialogue, which can make it easier to understand and manage emotions.

Metatron also serves as a guide on the journey of recovery from trauma, offering spiritual insights that aid healing. He can be invoked in therapies that integrate spiritual dimensions and work to heal both body and soul, helping individuals to overcome their past experiences and rebuild their lives.

Metatron promotes spiritual well-being as essential to overall mental health. He encourages people to cultivate a deep connection with the Divine, in whatever form this takes for the individual, and suggests that this connection can provide strength and comfort in the most difficult of times.

Metatron offers an invaluable spiritual toolkit for promoting mental health and well-being in an era of rapid change and ongoing challenges. His wisdom and guidance are a vital resource for those seeking to maintain sanity and serenity in a complex world.

In the digital age, where information and communication are faster and more accessible than ever before, Metatron is called upon to navigate the unique challenges of this new reality. He offers guidance on how to use technology to enrich one's spiritual life and foster genuine connections rather than superficiality and detachment.

Metatron teaches the importance of balancing online connection with meaningful face-to-face interactions. He warns of the dangers of digital isolation, where people can feel disconnected despite being constantly 'connected'. Metatron offers wisdom on how to maintain healthy relationships in both the digital and physical worlds.

Ethics in online communication is another aspect emphasised by Metatron. In an environment where anonymity can encourage harmful behaviour, he guides people to practice integrity and honesty in all their interactions, promoting a more respectful and constructive digital space.

Metatron promotes awareness of how digital content can affect both individuals and society. It advises on the responsibility of sharing information and the importance of checking facts before disseminating content, highlighting everyone's role in maintaining a healthy and trustworthy information environment.

Metatron shows how technology can be a powerful ally in spiritual growth. From meditation apps to spiritual discussion forums, he suggests ways to use digital tools to explore and expand spiritual awareness, making the spiritual path more accessible to everyone.

Metatron offers a valuable guide to meeting the challenges of the digital age with wisdom and integrity. He helps humanity to use technological tools in a way that promotes true connection, mutual understanding and spiritual development, ensuring that technology serves as an extension of human growth, not an obstacle.

Chapter Seventeen
Metatron's Eternal Legacy

Metatron, whose presence cuts across many traditions and cultures, serves as an archetype of the supreme spiritual leader. He is revered not only as an archangel or celestial being, but as a force that facilitates a deep understanding of the universe and the connection between the divine and the mundane.

Throughout this book we look at how Metatron is integrated into different spiritual practices around the world. He is a bridge between different faiths and philosophies, demonstrating that spiritual truth can transcend cultural and religious barriers. His teachings promote an inter-religious dialogue that enriches the understanding of all involved.

Metatron influences not only major events or cultural movements, but also the spiritual lives of individuals. He guides people on their personal journeys of self-discovery and spiritual growth, helping them to face personal challenges and achieve greater fulfilment and inner peace.

When considering the future of spirituality, the figure of Metatron emerges as a crucial guide for future generations. His legacy is seen as essential to the ongoing evolution of human consciousness, encouraging a constant search for knowledge, understanding and spiritual connection.

Metatron, as the "Angel of the Presence", is more than a mythological figure; he is a symbol of the human potential to transcend the tangible and touch the divine. Metatron's legacy reminds us that each of us carries the flame of spirituality which, when nurtured, can illuminate the darkest paths and bring meaning and purpose to our lives.

Reflecting on the teachings in this book, it becomes clear that Metatron offers more than simple spiritual guidance; he offers tools for deep, personal transformation. Each teaching and story associated with Metatron encourages us to look inward and discover our own spiritual paths with courage and dedication.

Metatron is not only a guide to heaven, but also to self-knowledge. His teachings encourage introspection and self-exploration, essential foundations for any spiritual journey. He helps people understand their own lights and shadows, and guides them through the process of enlightenment and soul cleansing.

One of Metatron's most powerful lessons is the importance of compassion and altruism. By living according to these principles, we learn not only to take better care of ourselves, but also to make a positive contribution to our community and environment, creating ripples of positive impact that extend far beyond our immediate actions.

Metatron teaches us that spirituality is not a solitary path. Through his influence we are encouraged to create and maintain spiritual communities that support the growth of all their members. These communities become refuges of peace, learning and mutual support, essential in a world that can often seem fragmented and isolated.

Reflecting on Metatron's teachings reaffirms the relevance of his wisdom in our world today. He teaches us that no matter what trials we face, there is always an opportunity for spiritual growth and renewal. Metatron's lessons continue to enlighten, inspire and challenge each of us to live a fuller and more spiritually engaged life.

Metatron not only guides people on their personal journeys, but also inspires spiritual leaders around the world. He serves as a role model for those who wish to lead with integrity, compassion and wisdom, and encourages them to cultivate communities that reflect these values. Metatron's influence is helping to shape a new generation of spiritual leaders committed to the collective wellbeing and evolution of human consciousness.

One of Metatron's most important contributions to future generations is his emphasis on spiritual education from an early age. He promotes programmes and initiatives that teach young people about the interconnectedness of all life forms and the importance of spiritual development. This education helps to instil lasting values of respect, love and responsibility.

Metatron is also considered a pioneer in the integration of technology and spirituality. He guides developers to create digital tools that promote meditation, mindfulness and spiritual study, making these practices more accessible to people of all ages and backgrounds. These technologies can help keep future generations connected to their spiritual traditions, even in an increasingly digital world.

Under Metatron's influence, future generations will be encouraged to adopt sustainable living practices that respect and protect the environment. Metatron teaches that caring for the planet is an extension of caring for one's own spirit, and this message resonates deeply with the young people who will lead environmental efforts in the future.

Metatron's legacy spans generations, providing a solid foundation for spiritual growth and responsible leadership. His influence on future generations promises the continuity of spiritual wisdom and a renewed commitment to the principles of interconnectedness, mutual respect and universal love. Metatron continues to be a source of inspiration and guidance for all who seek a more just and spiritually enriched world.

Metatron is celebrated in many different cultures and spiritual traditions, reflecting his ability to transcend boundaries and unite different faiths. He is an example of how spiritual principles can be universal, serving as a bridge that connects diverse spiritual and religious practices in search of common understanding.

In addition to his spiritual influence, Metatron also influences art and culture. He is a figure who inspires musicians, painters, writers and other artists to explore and express spiritual themes in their work. This influence helps to spread his message and teachings to a wider audience, expanding his presence and relevance.

Metatron promotes dialogue between different religions and spiritual practices, encouraging mutual understanding and respect. He is seen as a divine mediator, helping to overcome theological and cultural differences and promoting a more inclusive and harmonious vision of spirituality.

Metatron's legacy is perpetuated not only through sacred texts and transmitted teachings, but also through the collective memory of the communities that worship him. His figure is kept alive in the stories, rituals and practices that continue to inspire faith and devotion in successive generations.

Metatron transcends time and culture, serving as a beacon of wisdom and spiritual union. His ability to inspire and unite people from diverse backgrounds is a testament to his importance as a timeless and universal spiritual figure. He remains a symbol of how spirituality can transcend human divisions and unite humanity in pursuit of higher goals.

As we look to the future, Metatron's role as a spiritual guide remains crucial. He is seen as a compass for future generations, guiding them through spiritual and worldly challenges with wisdom and compassion. His influence is seen as essential to maintaining spiritual and ethical integrity in a world facing rapid change and increasing uncertainty.

As humanity enters an era of greater spiritual awareness, Metatron is being called upon to lead the way towards Ascension. He is a key figure in the transition to a new age of enlightenment in which spirituality is integrated into all aspects of human life, promoting a more harmonious and connected existence.

Metatron's legacy continues through the ongoing teaching of his truths and practices. Institutions, spiritual leaders and individuals committed to spiritual growth strive to keep his message alive and ensure that his wisdom continues to benefit humanity in meaningful ways.

Metatron continues to be a source of hope and renewal for those seeking spiritual guidance. In moments of despair or difficulty, his presence offers comfort and guidance, reminding us that every challenge is also an opportunity for spiritual growth and learning.

With his vast influence and profound wisdom, Metatron continues to be a guiding light for humanity's spiritual journey. His legacy is not only a testament to his own greatness, but an ongoing invitation for each of us to explore, understand and cultivate our own spiritual connections. He challenges us to live with purpose, to love deeply and to act with compassion, leading us towards a future in which spirituality and humanity are inextricably intertwined.

Chapter Eighteen
Techniques of Communication

This chapter is dedicated to spiritual enthusiasts who wish to improve their ability to connect and communicate with Metatron, the Archangel of Wisdom, Knowledge and Celestial Protection. Known for his divine closeness and power to intercede on behalf of human beings, Metatron serves as a spiritual guide, assisting in the development of a higher consciousness and a deeper understanding of the universe.

Before beginning any form of spiritual communication, it is essential to prepare an environment that leads to tranquillity and spiritual focus. This space serves as your personal sanctuary where distractions are minimised and energy flows freely.

Clean the environment:

Use coarse salt: Scatter coarse salt in the corners of the space where meditation and communication will take place. Salt is known for its cleansing and purifying properties and is able to absorb and neutralise negative energies.

White Sage: Burn white sage and allow the smoke to envelop the room. This "sage cleansing" ritual has been practiced for centuries by various indigenous cultures and is revered for its effectiveness in cleansing spaces of stagnant and impure energies.

Purifying sounds: Use instruments such as Tibetan bells or a singing bowl. The sound produced by these instruments is clear and resonant, and promotes purification of the environment through sound waves that are said to dissolve negative energy.

Create an altar:

Selecting objects: Choose items that symbolise your connection and intentions with Metatron. This may include crystals such as amethyst, known for its psychic cleansing and spiritual connection properties, and clear quartz, known to amplify intention and energy.

Prepare the altar: Set up a small table or shelf with a white or purple cloth representing spirituality and wisdom. Place the chosen crystals, an image or statue of Metatron if available, and any other personal items that represent your spiritual journey.

Light and scent: Add candles to illuminate the room with a soft light and use incense scents such as sandalwood or lavender, which help to relax the mind and deepen meditation.

By properly preparing the space, you have created a welcoming and sacred environment, a true sanctuary that facilitates connection with the Divine. This preparation is not only an essential part of the spiritual practice, but also a ritual that helps to centre the mind and heart, preparing them for the techniques of communicating with Metatron that will be explored in the next few pages of this chapter.

Meditation is a powerful tool for deepening spiritual communication. Through meditation we seek to achieve a state of mental clarity and spiritual openness that allows for a more intimate connection with Metatron. The following techniques are designed to attune your energy to that of the Archangel, thus facilitating a deeper and more meaningful spiritual dialogue.

1. Visualisation of Metatron:

Preparation: Begin with deep, slow breathing, sitting in a comfortable position with your back straight to facilitate the flow of energy. Close your eyes and imagine yourself in a space of pure white light, an environment that resonates with calm and peace.

Invocation of Metatron: With an open heart and mind, invoke Metatron and ask for his presence and guidance. Visualise a luminous figure in front of you, surrounded by a bright, radiant and welcoming light.

Communication: Concentrate on the figure of Metatron and open your heart to receive his messages. Ask what you need to know or understand better. Remain receptive and attentive to any thoughts, images or feelings that arise.

2. Use the Metatron Cube:

Understand the Cube: The Cube of Metatron, also known as the "Flower of Life", is a geometric shape made up of several circles and overlapping shapes that represent the interconnectedness of all things in the universe. It is a powerful symbol of protection and access to the Divine.

Visualisation of the Cube: During meditation, visualise the Cube of Metatron slowly descending from the heavens and positioning itself around you. See this cube rotating around you, activating and aligning your chakras, cleansing your energies and connecting you deeply to the Divine.

Interact with the Cube: As the cube rotates, imagine it attracting divine light and wisdom and channeling these energies to you. Feel enveloped by this energy, protected and guided by Metatron.

3. Final meditation:

Gratitude: After spending some time in meditation and communication with Metatron, thank him for his guidance and protection. Visualise Metatron's Cube rising back into the sky, leaving a trail of light.

Return to consciousness: Slowly bring your consciousness back to the physical space you are in. Wiggle your fingers and toes, stretch gently and open your eyes when you feel ready.

Recording experiences: It's useful to keep a spiritual journal nearby to record any insights or messages you receive during meditation. This can help you to understand and integrate Metatron's guidance into your daily life.

These meditation practices are not only techniques for achieving altered states of consciousness, but also ways of establishing a personal and ongoing relationship with Metatron. By incorporating these practices into your spiritual routine, you will develop a clearer and more direct communication with this powerful archangel, strengthening your spiritual journey and cosmic understanding.

The power of the spoken word is an essential tool for spiritual communication. Prayers and mantras can be used to invoke Metatron, establishing a direct and personal connection with the Archangel. These verbal practices help to focus the mind, harmonise energy and open the heart to receive divine wisdom.

1. Daily prayers to Metatron:

Morning Prayer for Guidance: Begin the day with a prayer asking Metatron to guide your actions and decisions. "Archangel Metatron, who dwells near the divine throne, guide me with your light and wisdom. Protect my steps and illuminate my path this coming day.

Night prayer for protection: Before going to sleep, call upon Metatron to protect you and your space during the night. "Heavenly guardian Metatron, surround me tonight with your protective aura. Guard my rest and ward off all evil.

2. Mantras of power:

Spiritual Cleansing Mantra: Use this mantra to cleanse your room and aura of negative energies. Repeat seven times: "Metatron, cleanse and release, bring harmony and peace".

Divine Connection Mantra: To strengthen your connection with the Divine, recite: "Metatron, celestial mediator, connect me to wisdom and eternal light.

3. Metatron Invocation Ritual:

Ritual Preparation: Choose a time and place where you won't be disturbed. Prepare the room as described above and have a clear quartz crystal or amethyst handy.

Invocation process: Light a white candle and hold the crystal. Visualise a golden light enveloping the room and recite the following invocation: "Archangel Metatron, who serves as a bridge between the Earth and the Divine, I call upon your sacred presence to guide and enlighten my spiritual journey".

Meditation and Communication: After the invocation, meditate on Metatron's presence, opening yourself to any messages or sensations. Talk to Metatron as if you were talking to a wise mentor.

4. Automatic writing exercises:

Introduction to automatic writing: After a meditation session, take a notebook and quickly write down whatever comes to mind, without judgement. This may include messages perceived during the meditation.

Interpretation and reflection: Review what you have written, looking for patterns or specific messages that may have been communicated by Metatron.

The use of prayers, mantras and rituals is a powerful way of strengthening your connection with Metatron. These practices not only facilitate communication with the Archangel, but also help you to integrate his guidance and protection into your daily life. With dedication and regular practice, you will develop a deeper and more meaningful relationship with Metatron, enriching your spiritual journey.

Rituals are structured ceremonies that use symbols, objects and specific intentions to facilitate deeper communication with the Divine. This chapter explores detailed rituals that will help you communicate directly with Metatron, allowing for an enriching spiritual dialogue and a more intimate connection.

1. Spiritual Cleansing Ritual:

Purpose: To cleanse the room and the practitioner of negative energies, preparing them for clear communication with Metatron.

Materials needed: White sage or palo santo, rock salt, holy water and a white candle.

Procedure:

Start by physically cleaning the place where the ritual will take place.

Sprinkle coarse salt in the corners of the room and along the windows and doors.

Light the sage or palo santo and walk around the room to purify every corner.

Use the holy water to sprinkle in the four corners of the room and on yourself.

Light the white candle in the centre of the room and meditate briefly, asking Metatron to cleanse and protect the environment.

2. Rite of passage with Metatron:

Purpose: To facilitate a significant transition in the practitioner's life, be it a new beginning, a career change or a profound spiritual development.

Materials Required: Clear quartz and amethyst crystals, sandalwood incense and an image or symbol of Metatron.

Procedure:

Prepare your altar with the crystals, the image of Metatron and the incense.

Light the incense and concentrate on the rising smoke, visualising it as a link between you and the Divine.

Hold the crystals in your hands while saying a prayer asking Metatron to guide and support you during this period of transformation.

Meditate on the changes you wish to make and visualise Metatron giving you the courage and clarity you need to move forward.

Finish the ritual by thanking Metatron for his guidance and protection and keep the crystals as a physical reminder of the Archangel's presence in your life.

3. Festivals and celebrations in honour of Metatron:

Aim: To integrate the worship of Metatron into celebrations and festivals that bring spiritual communities together to strengthen bonds and share experiences.

Celebration ideas:

Organise a community gathering on significant dates associated with Metatron, such as the equinox or solstice.

Create workshops or sharing circles where people can learn more about Metatron and share devotional practices.

Hold light ceremonies in which candles are lit to symbolise Metatron's enlightenment and wisdom.

These rituals are a powerful way to honour and invoke Metatron's presence in your life. They not only strengthen your spiritual connection, but also allow you to interact more consciously and directly with this Archangel. With regular practice, you will find that your ability to perceive and interpret Metatron's guidance will become clearer and more accurate.

Maintaining an ongoing connection with Metatron can transform daily spirituality into a source of strength, clarity and inspiration. This page explores how to incorporate daily practices that honour Metatron, and how these practices can help to maintain constant and fruitful communication with this archangel.

1. Morning with Metatron:

Morning Meditation: Begin the day with a short meditation focusing on visualising Metatron and his bright light. Ask for guidance and protection for the day ahead.

Morning Prayer: Recite a prayer dedicated to Metatron, asking for wisdom and energy to face the challenges of the day. It can be a simple prayer such as: "Metatron, guide me with your light; protect me with your strength; light my way with your wisdom".

2. Nights with Metatron:

Review of the day: Before you go to sleep, do a brief review of your day. Reflect on the moments when you felt Metatron's presence and thank him for any help or insight you received.

Evening prayer: Close the day with a prayer thanking Metatron for his protection and guidance. Ask for a peaceful and restful sleep, free from worry and negative energies.

3. Create a personal altar:

Altar of Metatron: Set aside a place in your home for a personal altar to Metatron. Include images, symbols (such as the Metatron Cube), crystals associated with him and other items that you feel connect you to the Archangel.

Altar maintenance: Regularly clean and reorganise the altar to reflect your intentions and gratitude to Metatron. This sacred space will serve as a focal point for your daily practices and meditations.

4. Incorporate Metatron into your daily life:

Decisions and intuitions: Whenever you are faced with important decisions, ask Metatron for clarity and guidance. Watch for intuitions and signs that may be answers to your prayers.

Protection on journeys: Before embarking on any journey, whether physical or spiritual, invoke Metatron for protection and safety during the journey.

5. Sharing experiences and fellowship:

Study and meditation groups: Join or organise study and meditation groups focused on Metatron.

Sharing experiences with others can enrich your personal practice and offer new perspectives.

Teaching and learning: Be a channel for teaching others about Metatron and its practices. Sharing your knowledge and experience can help others find their own spiritual path.

Integrating Metatron into your daily life not only strengthens your spiritual connection, but also transforms your daily experience, filling it with greater purpose and clarity. Regular practice and the maintenance of an altar are fundamental to cultivating a lasting and deep relationship with Metatron, allowing you to live each day under his divine guidance and protection.

Chapter Nineteen
Prayers and Rituals

In this chapter we explore devotional practices centred on prayers and rituals dedicated to Metatron, the Archangel of immense power and wisdom. These practices are fundamental for those who seek spiritual guidance, protection and a deeper connection to the divine through the worship of Metatron.

Specific prayers to Metatron

The power of prayer is immense, acting as a direct channel of communication with the Divine. Here are prayers formulated to invoke Metatron for different needs and moments of the day.

Prayer for protection:

"Archangel Metatron, protector of the heavenly realms, I ask you to surround me and my loved ones with your protective light. Protect us from all evil and guide us in safety and peace.

Prayer for wisdom and guidance:

"O Metatron, archangel of divine wisdom, enlighten my mind with your heavenly knowledge. Help me to see clearly and to make decisions that reflect the true light of understanding and love.

Morning prayer to begin the day:

"Dear Metatron, as I begin this day, I place myself under your spiritual guidance. May every step I take be grounded in your presence and may every decision I make be inspired by your heavenly wisdom.

Evening Prayer for Gratitude and Peace:

"As the day draws to a close, I thank you, Metatron, for your guidance and protection. Allow me to rest in peace under your watchful eye and recharge my spirit for the coming dawn.

These prayers can be said daily or at specific times of need. They are designed to strengthen your connection with Metatron and ensure his constant and beneficial presence in your life.

Rituals are ceremonies that use physical and spiritual elements to create an environment conducive to communication with the Divine. This section offers detailed rituals that can help you to establish a deeper connection with Metatron, facilitating an enriching spiritual dialogue.

1. Ritual of Spiritual Purification and Protection:

Purpose: This ritual aims to cleanse the environment and the practitioner of negative influences, thus creating a sacred space for communication with Metatron.

Materials needed: Coarse salt, holy water, white sage or palo santo, white candle.

Procedure:

Begin by physically cleaning the place of practice.

Sprinkle coarse salt in the corners of the room to purify and protect the space.

Light the sage or palo santo and pass the smoke around the room, concentrating on cleansing and protection.

Use the holy water to sprinkle in the shape of a cross in each corner and at the entrance to the room.

Light the white candle in the centre of the room and dedicate it to Metatron as a symbol of divine light.

2. Ritual of direct communication with Metatron:

Purpose: To facilitate clear and direct communication with Metatron, seeking guidance or answers to specific questions.

Materials needed: Paper, pen, two white candles, incense of myrrh or frankincense.

Procedure:

Prepare the ritual space, making sure it is clean and quiet.

Light the candles and incense to create a meditative atmosphere.

Write down a specific question or request to Metatron.

Meditate for a few minutes, concentrating on your intention and Metatron's presence.

Burn the paper in the flame of one of the candles, visualising your message being delivered directly to Metatron.

Thank Metatron for his guidance and end the ritual by blowing out the candles and collecting the materials used.

3. Ritual of thanks and closure:

Purpose: To thank Metatron for the communication and to keep the door open for future interactions.

Materials needed: Quartz crystals, a blue candle, white flowers.

Procedure:

Place the crystals and flowers around the blue candle.

Light the candle and verbally express your gratitude to Metatron for the messages and protection you have received.

Offer the flowers as a symbol of gratitude and respect.

Keep the crystals in a visible place as a reminder of Metatron's continued presence in your life.

These rituals not only strengthen your connection with Metatron, but also enrich your spiritual practice by providing moments of introspection and divine communication. They can be adapted and repeated as needed, each contributing to a deeper and more meaningful relationship with the Archangel.

Celebrations and festivals are powerful moments for the community to come together and honour the spiritual forces. This section shows how to organise and participate in events dedicated to Metatron, helping to strengthen community bonds and deepen the spiritual connection.

1. Planning Celebrations in Honour of Metatron

Choosing dates: Choose dates that have spiritual significance, such as solstices or equinoxes, which are traditionally times of change and renewal.

Theme of the celebration: Define a theme that resonates with Metatron's attributes, such as 'Divine Wisdom' or 'Heavenly Protection'.

2. Organise the event:

Venue: Choose a place that offers a peaceful and welcoming atmosphere, preferably outdoors, so that participants can feel closer to nature and the elements.

Decoration: Use symbols associated with Metatron, such as the Cube of Metatron or the Flower of Life, in banners and decorations. Include colours such as white and light blue, which symbolise purity and spirituality.

Activities: Plan activities that promote meditation, communal prayer, chanting and sacred dancing to create an immersive and spiritual experience.

3. Community Rituals:

Opening ceremony: Begin the festival with an opening ceremony that includes cleansing the space with sage or palo santo and a collective invocation to Metatron.

Guided meditation: Conduct a guided meditation that allows participants to visualise and connect with Metatron, asking for his guidance and blessings.

Offerings and thanks: Encourage participants to bring offerings, such as flowers or crystals, which can be placed on a temporary altar. Close with a ceremony of thanksgiving, acknowledging Metatron's presence and help.

4. Community integration and sharing:

Sharing circle: After the rituals, form a sharing circle in which participants can share their experiences and insights gained during the event.

Communal meal: Organise a time of fellowship with light and healthy food that promotes community and sharing among participants.

Celebrating Metatron through festivals not only strengthens the individual connection with the divine, but also builds a spiritually engaged community. These events serve as powerful reminders of Metatron's ongoing support and guidance, and of how spirituality can be experienced collectively.

Incorporating Metatron into your daily routine is a powerful way to maintain a constant connection and receive ongoing guidance. This section offers simple but effective practices that can be incorporated into daily life to strengthen your relationship with this archangel.

1. Mornings with Metatron:

Morning Meditation: Take a few minutes each morning to meditate in Metatron's presence. Visualise his light surrounding you and guiding your actions throughout the day.

Prayer of Intention: Say a morning prayer asking Metatron to guide your decisions and illuminate your path with wisdom and understanding.

2. Moments of reflection throughout the day:

Pause to breathe: In moments of stress or decision, take short breaks to breathe deeply and call upon Metatron. Ask for clarity and serenity to face the challenges.

Notes and Insights: Keep a spiritual diary to record any insights or messages you feel Metatron is giving you throughout the day.

3. Nights with Metatron:

Nightly review: Before going to sleep, review the day and reflect on how Metatron's presence may have influenced various situations. Give thanks for his guidance and protection.

Night Prayer: End the day with a prayer thanking Metatron for his company and asking for a peaceful and restful night's rest.

4. Make a personal altar to Metatron:

Prepare the altar: In a quiet corner of your home, create an altar dedicated to Metatron. Include images or symbols that represent the Archangel, such as the Metatron Cube or the Flower of Life.

Regular maintenance: Maintain the altar regularly, cleaning and rearranging items as necessary to keep the energy fresh and vibrant.

5. Participation in spiritual communities:

Study and meditation groups: Join local or online groups that focus on the study of the archangels, or Metatron in particular. Sharing experiences can enrich your personal practice.

Events and ceremonies: Attend events or ceremonies that celebrate Metatron. These are opportunities to connect with other devotees and deepen your spiritual understanding.

Daily practices with Metatron help to create a spiritual structure in your life, bringing clarity, protection and guidance. These practices not only enrich your spiritual journey, but also provide ongoing comfort and support, making each day more meaningful and purposeful.

Sharing your experience and knowledge of Metatron not only helps to spread his worship, but also strengthens your own spiritual connection by teaching and learning from others. This section offers guidelines on how to educate and inspire others to connect with Metatron.

1. Organise study and discussion groups:

Form groups: Form or join study groups that focus on angels and archangels, with a particular emphasis on Metatron. These groups can meet regularly to discuss texts, share experiences and meditate together.

Discussion topics: Include topics such as the history of Metatron, his portrayal in different spiritual traditions and techniques for communicating with him.

2. Holding workshops or seminars:

Event planning: Organise workshops or seminars on Metatron, teaching meditation techniques, prayer and other communication rituals.

Teaching materials: Developing teaching materials, such as booklets or digital presentations, that summarise the main points about Metatron and give practical instructions.

3. Creation of online content:

Blogs and articles: Write detailed blogs or articles about your experiences with Metatron, exploring different aspects of his spiritual influence.

Videos and Podcasts: Produce videos or podcasts that can reach a wider audience, discussing topics related to Metatron and sharing guided meditations or inspirational readings.

4. Attend spiritual fairs and events:

Spiritual Fairs: Participate in spiritual fairs and events as an exhibitor, offering information and materials about Metatron.

Public lectures: Use these opportunities to give talks or conduct ceremonies that introduce Metatron to new audiences, explaining his role and how to invoke him.

5. Create a community of support:

Social networking: Use social networking sites to create an online community where people interested in Metatron can connect, share experiences and support each other.

Regular meetings: Organise regular meetings, physical or virtual, to strengthen the community and allow members to share their spiritual journeys and personal growth.

Sharing the knowledge and worship of Metatron not only broadens understanding and devotion to this powerful archangel, but also enriches your own spiritual experience. By educating others, you reaffirm your commitment to the spiritual path and help to create a network of enlightened and supportive individuals.

Epilogue

As I conclude this journey through the pages of The Book of Metatron, I would like to express my deep gratitude to all of you who have immersed yourselves in this inspiring narrative. It has been an honour to share this quest for divine wisdom and to reveal the secrets of the Archangel Metatron, the celestial mediator that connects us to the Creator.

My sincere thanks to all the readers who, with open hearts, have allowed themselves to be touched by the words, stories and teachings contained within. May this book have given you new perspectives, enlightenment and a deep sense of peace and purpose.

Thank you also to all those dedicated souls who, in their never-ending quest for spiritual knowledge and understanding, keep the flame of faith alive and inspire others to find their own spiritual journey. They are the essence of this book.

To all the scholars, mystics and seekers who have contributed to the understanding of Metatron over the centuries, my gratitude is eternal. Your discoveries, visions and revelations have brought us closer to divine truths and without your efforts this work would not have been possible.

Finally, I thank Metatron, the Archangel, who dwells among us as a beacon of light and wisdom. May his blessings continue to guide us and may his heavenly presence inspire our lives and lead us to a deeper understanding of our purpose and the divine light that dwells within us all.

May each of you continue to find guidance, protection and healing on your spiritual journey. May Metatron's blessings always be with you and may his wisdom enlighten your hearts and minds.

Infinite gratitude and radiant blessings.

www.ingramcontent.com/pod-product-compliance
Lightning Source LLC
LaVergne TN
LVHW040057080526
838202LV00045B/3679